WRITING FOR YOUNG CHILDREN is addressed to writers and would-be writers for children. But in facing the problem of writing books that are satisfying to children, Claudia Lewis faces problems that concern all who enjoy or seek to understand children and all who enjoy or seek to understand the art of language. Claudia Lewis brings to her subject the rare combination of a scientist and an artist. She has sought to understand children both as a teacher and as a research worker in psychology and ethnology.

Claudia Lewis says that William Steig, Maurice Sendak, and others have created fantastic worlds equal to the great books by E. B. White, A. A. Milne, and other masters of children's literature. The object remains the same: "The author who puts himself, or the child in himself, into a story written for children will inevitably reach that listening adult at the other end. For all of us, though grown, still hope and wait, childlike, to hear those words that will touch us."

WRITING FOR YOUNG CHILDREN, first published in 1954 and hailed as a classic work in the field, is now back in print with a revised, updated bibliography and a new epilogue by the author. Lucy Sprague Mitchell writes in the Foreword: "It is a book about children and how their language reveals what is going on inside them about language and how to make stories for children that will heighten and deepen their satisfaction."

Claudia Lewis has long been associated with the Bank Street College of Education, as a member of both the teaching and research staffs. She is the author of many books for children as well as a book that teaches children to write. She received her Ph.D. from Columbia University and has taught children in special workshops across the country.

WRITING FOR YOUNG CHILDREN

By the same author
Children of the Cumberland

CLAUDIA LEWIS

Writing for Young Children

ANCHOR PRESS/DOUBLEDAY
GARDEN CITY, NEW YORK
1981

Writing for Young Children was originally published in hardcover by Simon & Schuster, Inc., 1954.

Anchor Books edition: 1981

ISBN: 0-385-15392-9
Library of Congress Catalog Card Number: 79-6588

Grateful acknowledgment is made to students, children, parents, schools, for use of original stories and exercises.

Thanks to the following for use of copyrighted material:

From *Charlotte's Web*, by E. B. White. Copyright 1952 by E. B. White. Courtesy of Harper & Row, Publishers, Inc.

From *The Little House in the Big Woods*, by Laura Ingalls Wilder. Copyright 1932, as to text, by Laura Ingalls Wilder. Renewed 1959 by Roger L. MacBride. Courtesy of Harper & Row, Publishers, Inc.

From *The Runaway Bunny*, by Margaret Wise Brown. Copyright 1942 by Harper & Row, Publishers, Inc. Text renewed © 1970 by Roberta Brown Rauch. By permission of Harper & Row, Publishers, Inc.

"Mrs. Peck Pigeon," from *Eleanor Farjeon's Poems for Children*, by Eleanor Farjeon. Originally published in *Over the Garden Wall*. Copyright 1933, 1961 by Eleanor Farjeon. By permission of J. B. Lippincott Co.

Excerpts from *The Quiet Noisy Book*, by Margaret Wise Brown. Copyright 1950 by Margaret Wise Brown. Renewed 1978 by Roberta Brown Rauch and Leonard Weisgard. Reprinted by permission of Harper & Row, Publishers, Inc.

Excerpts from *The House at Pooh Corner*, by A. A. Milne. Copyright 1928 by E. P. Dutton & Co., Inc. Copyright renewal 1956 by A. A. Milne. Excerpts from *When We Were Very Young*, by A. A. Milne. Copyright 1924 by E. P. Dutton & Co., Inc. Copyright renewed 1952, by A. A. Milne. Both reprinted by permission of the publisher, E. P. Dutton & Co., Inc.

"The Dance," by William Carlos Williams, *The Collected Later Poems*. Copyright 1944 by William Carlos Williams. Reprinted by permission of New Directions Publishing Corp.

To
LUCY SPRAGUE MITCHELL
A pioneer in the field of writing
for children—
And a great teacher

CONTENTS

FOREWORD

Writing for Young Children is a book to enjoy and to learn from. It is a book about children and how their language reveals what is going on inside them; about language and how to make stories for children that will heighten and deepen their satisfactions. It is addressed primarily to writers and would-be writers for children. But in facing the problem of writing books that are satisfying to children, Claudia Lewis faces problems that concern all who enjoy or seek to understand children and all who enjoy or seek to understand the art of language. Readers of *Writing for Young Children* will, I believe, develop more sensitive, listening ears and an experimental attitude—be they teachers or parents, or writers or artists who deal with media other than language, or those who simply enjoy children or language. For the author has skillfully woven the strands—children and language—into a pattern that holds both meaning and charm. Her book makes good reading. Her own language as she develops this pattern exemplifies how the significance of ideas can be clarified and heightened by delight in the language through which the ideas are presented.

Claudia Lewis brings to her subject the rare combination of a scientist and an artist. She has sought to understand children both as a teacher and as a research worker in psychology and ethnology. Her continuing interest in the arts has led her both to writing verse for children and articles on the quality of children's language and, as a staff member of the Bank Street College of Education, to giving courses for people who want to write and for those preparing to teach children. In addition, for her own satisfaction she has worked in many fields of art other than writing—in music, painting, and the dance.

This broad and varied experience from which Claudia Lewis speaks makes this book like a window through which people of differing interests will catch new vistas, new insights that will add to their understanding and their pleasure in the world they live in.

The opening page of her Introduction reveals the method she pursues throughout her book. She begins by quoting questions asked by a seven-year-old girl: "How do people feel when they are grown up? Do they feel tall and fat? Do they feel all finished?" This quotation is direct evidence. It takes us immediately behind a child's eyes where we can look out from a child's world at her surprising image of adults—ourselves. It shocks us into a realization of the immense gap between the immediacy and poignancy with which a child feels his physical self and our adult atrophy of the kinesthetic feeling. It sets the stage for exploring what children are like from direct evidence furnished by their language. It sets the stage for exploring what an adult must learn about children in order to meet them in *their* world—not in an adult world. And it also sets the stage for the special subject of this book—writing for young children. This comment by a child, says Miss Lewis, "is a children's language, and a writer's language; one to learn from, whether we call ourselves juvenile writers, fiction writers, poets."

Such is the author's method throughout the book: Presenting direct evidence through remarks of children in which they unconsciously reveal what is going on inside them, and then using these remarks as a basis for discussion of techniques of writing that will present the world of people and things as it looks, sounds, and *feels* to children.

Yes, this is a book centered around writing for children. But I believe that the approach the author has used, based as it is on what children are like, makes this book invaluable to all people who are concerned with children and their growth. All parents and teachers use language in their relationships with their children and all children, after the prelanguage stage, use language both for communication and for their own pleasure. Parents and teachers, quite as much as writers, need sensitive listening ears really to hear what children say and an understanding interpretation of children's remarks to guide their replies. Parents and teachers could profitably substitute "talk with children" for "writing for children" throughout this book. They, too, would learn from an experimental approach to their own adult language in talking with children. They, too, need to know "what children are looking for" and to resolve in their own minds the "fantasy-reality question" which arises often in everyday life with children. Obviously, the challenging thinking in this book may help adults, unless they are really "all finished," to build criteria upon which they choose books for their children. Is it not equally obvious that this kind of thinking may help in answering children's questions and in deciding what questions to raise with them? Language *by* children gives a significant insight into their inner feeling and interests: language used by adults *with* children is a significant tool for meeting children "where they live."

I cannot forbear to say one more word about my pleasure in this book. Not only do I enjoy this book because it deals with the matters upon which my own professional work has been centered—children, adults who work with children, and language. I enjoy it also from a more personal angle. It brings me the satisfaction that a teacher has in watching a one-time student of hers grow in breadth and depth of thinking and in power to express that thinking. Claudia Lewis has written a book that I should be proud to have written. As it is, I am proud of the small share I had when she was a student at the School for Teachers at the Bank Street College in helping her to develop her great native gifts and work on interests that I have seen expand and grow until they could produce a book such as this.

Lucy Sprague Mitchell

New York, February, 1954

AUTHOR'S PREFACE
TO THE NEW EDITION

What should I say about this little book that is now twenty-five years old? Would I write it today in the same way? How much of it would I like to change and how much of it have I changed for the new edition?

The reader will find that I am letting the book stand just as I wrote it, with the exception of removing throughout the text the names of a few old books that are no longer easily available and substituting newer ones. I am updating the bibliographies and adding a chapter at the end to bring the reader into our present scene. That is all. I have not even felt it advisable to cut up the text in order to say "he/she" or "they" instead of "he." I expect the reader to assume, along with me, that the masculine pronoun can be construed in more than a literal sense.

So, this is essentially the old *Writing for Young Children*. Yet I don't feel that it is "old." For it says today what I still want to say, what I still believe in. Reading the book over, I surprise myself, coming upon thoughts that I might have written only yesterday. True, our trends and our fashions change, but contemporary writers who have something lasting to say to children are in many respects very little different from those writers of long ago whose books are still on the shelves, still pleasing children. All have held a few things in common. What these are has been my task in this book to try to pinpoint, though I have known, of course, that there is no single key to unlock those doors that so many of us hope to open.

INTRODUCTION

Primer Lesson

"How do people feel when they are grown up? Do they feel tall and fat? Do they feel all finished?"

When I came upon this query by a little girl, aged seven, recorded on scratch paper in a teacher's hasty handwriting, I said to myself, This takes me straight to the point I have been trying to make for years in my workshop for juvenile writers. No doubt about it, *children know how they feel,* inside and out, from their toenails to their teeth, while we grownups—and would-be writers at that—have long since lost contact with our physical selves. Oh, we know that we have headaches, backaches, fallen arches—yes. But tallness and fatness, or their equivalent, no. This child's comment strikes upon our blunt ears like a language from another time and place.

It is a children's language, and a writer's language, one to learn from, whether we call ourselves juvenile writers, fiction writers, poets, storytellers.

It is a writer's language because it springs from lively sensory perception, and is for that reason evocative and fresh. It is a language close to the living source. ("Original" means just that.)

The child speaks this language because he is by nature a kinesthetic creature, tapping the world through feeling, touch, sight, and sound.

In his early encounters with our adult speech, he is bewildered by abstractions or metaphors one step removed from concrete experience. Ask him, "Did you have difficulty this morning?" and he may answer, "No, I had an egg." Comment upon what sharp eyes he has, and you may only disturb him. "My eyes don't have points on them!"

He puts the world together for himself, bit by bit, touching, reaching, trying, an explorer pushing back his concentric horizons with his own hands. "Suède feels like liver." "When your foot's asleep it feels like cracker crumbs." "Oh!"—upon seeing blue grapes for the first time— "blueberries on the cob!"

He has not had time yet to learn the conventions we adults lag among. Ask a five-year-old to tell you what the "easiest thing in the world" is, and it isn't likely that he'll say anything about pumpkin pie, nor do such stereotyped expressions as "Slow as a snail," and "Quiet as a mouse," belong in his early vocabulary. Instead, an "easy" thing to him is "Easy as when you wash your face in the morning your cheeks get red." He can still think and talk in terms of "Slow as your new teeth come in," and "Quiet as a thermometer goes up." He comes racing in from watching a parade: "I saw a man with a big big drum, from his knees up to his neck!" His *eyes* measure the world around him. He has not yet taken over those wooden rulers we try to foist upon him. "The bread in the toaster just stayed bread," he tells us, as he tries to explain that the electricity is not working at his house. And with simple, honest acknowledgment of what it feels like, in his young responsive body, to stand in the presence of new-fallen snow, he reports: "The snow was very very deep, and I said, 'How nice it looks,' and so I lay down in it."

Secret wish of us all, but how we cast it from us. Tall, fat, and finished. No more lying in deep snow to test the weight, to feel the softness, to wrap ourselves round in snowy texture. No. The snow is "beautiful." Let it go at that.

Yet the urge tweaks at us. It is there. Beneath our protective coverings, we, too, have nerves and muscles, eyes to see with, a body to roll in snow with.

If we could just take ourselves by the collar and shake the sterile wooden pencils from our hands. . . .

Begin by tearing off those top layers of yours, I say to the students who come to learn "how to write for children," and to the parents and teachers who want to learn more about the art of communicating with children. You, too, have your own perceptions, your own feelings. Take some experience that was vivid to you—pleasant, exhilarating, frightening, anything that had strong sensations connected with it. Now forget these adjectives that I have just used, these nondescript borrowed words. What really happened to you? And by "you" I mean the breathing, balance-loving body of you, with its two movable legs and arms, its emotion-registering stomach, its need of warmth and dread of cold, its marvelous perceiving eyes.

Try a familiar summer vacation experience like lying in the sun on the beach. (Forget "lazy," "restful.") See how the telling of it can jump into life, as a child's telling is alive, when we keep the words close to the sun and sand as we felt them:

> I spread my white, blanket-sized towel on the dry, deep, and hot sand and stretch out on my stomach. I feel the sand move and grind under me as I mold the towel into it with my body. I feel the sun reach down to find me. It slowly, gradually heats every part of my body until I think I feel myself turning brown at the edges. It beats insistently until it draws out droplets of perspiration that crawl down my cheeks and down the creases of my neck. I feel them in back of my knees and under my arms. I touch my back and my arms, and they are as hot as the sand around me. I slowly turn over and sit up, squinting at the brilliant whiteness of the sand and the brightness of the sea. Then a light sea breeze stirs and touches me, and I am refreshed and cool again. Now I lie back. I mold my body into the sand again, and my face points up at the orange heat above me. The sun heats my body until the strength crawls out of my arms through my fingers and out of my legs through my toes.

Or take a common thing like gardening:

> I made the rows with my fingers, letting the earth cover my hands and get under my nails. Soon my

, hands would feel very dry, as though the skin were being pulled tightly toward my wrist.

Yes, we say, the dry skin, it *is* like that; how is it we had forgotten!

Obviously we have become too used to our skin. Yet when someone says, See here, remember that feeling at the wrist, then the dormant past stirs in us, disturbingly.

It is through our wrists and hands, our eyes and ears— through our tallness and fatness, if you will—that we find our way to vitality of word and thought. This is the primer lesson for the writer, and the teacher is the child himself.

"Brother Find Brother!" we used to chant, when a ball was lost, and we flung another out to retrieve it. . . .

There will be time enough to consider the questions of what to write, and how to avoid the pitfalls of the craft, after we have equipped ourselves with the child's own coin.

He listens to those who speak his language. It is a language of action, of sensory images, a language telling of the touch of things, and their colors, odors, sounds.

It has movement, pace, rhythm. For the child is not a static creature. Out of his reservoir of sensory responsiveness come rushing up the words that move with the rhythm of his thought; galloping, bumping, coasting, swinging words. How does the choppy sea go? Why, "Wibbly, woobly, dabbly, dubbly, bibbly," of course. And the child dances this as he speaks it. Rhythm of sounds, rhythm of movement, these are one.

Exercises used as examples throughout this book were written by students in the Language Arts courses at Bank Street College of Education. They are presented not as models to be copied, nor as illustrations of expert use of language, but rather as examples of first steps a beginning writer can take for himself.

Kipling spoke this language of imagery and sound, and children do not forget the "great grey-green greasy Limpopo River, all set about with fever-trees." They go back again and again to the storyteller who talks with the live words tumbling, as it seems, from his mouth: "In the High and Far-Off Times the Elephant, O Best Beloved, had no trunk."

They go back to Kenneth Grahame, for the sake of the little Mole who "scraped and scratched and scrabbled and scrooged" till he popped up into the sunlight. They go back, too, for the sake of that very sunshine, striking hot on the fur, and for the sake of the little Mole "jumping off all his four legs at once, in the joy of living."

The youngest ones recognize their language with delight when they hear it in the loved refrain of *The Little Engine That Could:* "I think I can, I think I can, I think I can . . ."

They are drawn back to the old folk tales, too, by the power of the rhythmical repeated word: "No, no, by the hair of my chinny-chin-chin." . . . " 'Very well then,' said the Little Red Hen, 'I will.' And she did." . . . "I am the gingerbread man, I am I am." . . .

Whenever the writer can seize upon a phrase of living speech; whenever he can make us feel the hot sun on our backs, or dampness against the skin, or light and dark around us; when he can make us see his characters kicking up their heels; whenever he can strike out sounding and rhythmical clinks, snaps, thumps, from the black print letters, children will listen, and will return to listen again.

Is there nothing more to it? Is this *all* children want?

No, of course they want a great deal more. A story that offers only a succession of vivid words and images—sound without content, or plot or plan or surprise—is scarcely a story at all. And a distinction must be made between what the three-year-old wants and what the eight-year-old wants.

Children, however, are not to be thought of as any less receptive than adults to language that is art as well as communication. Primarily they want what we all want when we open a book—words that can work a little magic, a language strong enough to hold emotion.

The juvenile writer's first step is to become aware of the kind of words he is putting together. His first step is to ask himself, "Is there any life in what I am writing?"

The vitality—or "art"—of language, as children so clearly show us, has to do with the writer's ability to make use of his own wellsprings—of the feelings and perceptions that lie within his own live orbit.

WRITING FOR YOUNG CHILDREN

CHAPTER I

The Language
of Sensory Perception

It is not always easy for us to learn to use again a concrete, personal language, though we were skillful at it in our primer days.

How do the children do it? Let us remind ourselves once again: The child tells us *what a thing feels like:*

Age 3:

This high hill makes my legs feel like bending.

Age 6:

Song of the River

Oh my heavy load,
My heavy load,
I cannot hold,
I cannot hold.

When the wind blows,
Waves go rustling over me.
I shiver,
I'm cold.
It ripples so, it itches me.

Age 8:

The Bridge

The bridge is a long arm and he stretches his long arm way across the river and I think it is beautiful. The cars go bumpty, bumpty, bump and the streetcars go over it. And his fingers just touch the other side, and his back must ache sometimes, but he never lets go for he knows that it would do some damage. So he never lets go and he looks down under him and he sees the boats go under him and at night he goes to sleep. And pretty soon a boat comes and the bridge has to wake up. And the boat goes toot-toot-tooting and that is the way his life goes.

Age 9:

Morning Air

Sometimes I go out of doors before breakfast. In the early morning, the air is fresher than further on in the day. You can smell pine trees, box hedges, and flowers. When I go in, breakfast smells so good!

Age 7:

Spring
(Dictated by a group of children)

Flowers are blooming in spring, and the trees and the birds. Grass grows green. Butterflies are in the air. Trees are growing, and potatoes and carrots and lettuce and celery and onions and beets. It gets warmer and we all go swimming. We put on summer clothes. Children are playing in the nice sunshiny day. The sun shines on the brooks. We begin to eat strawberries for breakfast, and raspberries. The farmer begins to drive out the cows and the horses and the sheep and the chickens. All fruits begin to blossom, all fruit blossoms that there are. Pears begin to grow. Nearly every night I go over to the bay to see the boats sailing. The trees get sort of flower leaves. You pick them off and take them home. Little birdies drink of the spring. Children rollerskate in the park. I take pictures through the trees. Morning-glories grow and blossom. The daisies begin to bloom, and roses and violets.

The three-year-old, climbing his high hill, has not learned to say that it "tires" his legs. In his simple statement of what actually happens to him lies the key to the growing power of his language.

The six-year-old, writing so vividly of the river, becomes a river. He does not stand on the shore and watch, detached, like a recording machine on the banks. He *is* the river, sensing its weight and movement. His skin is alive to

it. And in the same way the child who describes the bridge
is not vacantly describing. He reaches, with the bridge. His
way of looking includes stretching with the arm, touching
with the finger tips. Eyesight is not yet cut off from body
sight. What Louis Danz, in *Personal Revolution and
Picasso*, said of the artist might well be said of the child:
"The eyes are merely holes for the body to feel through."

The nine-year-old, writing of the morning air, scarcely
relies upon his eyes at all. He lets the fresh morning air
come through to us on the sense of smell.

And what are the seven-year-olds doing in their spring
song, except telling us how their young live bodies know it
is spring? They think in terms of the simple concrete
things—the strawberries and beets, the skates, the flowers
on the trees.

There was another singer of spring once, centuries ago,
whose words we still repeat.

> For lo, the winter is past, the rain is over and gone;
>   The flowers appear on the earth; the time of the
> singing of birds is come, and the voice of the turtle is
> heard in our land.
>   The fig tree putteth forth her green figs, and the
> vines with the tender grape give a good smell. Arise,
> my love, my fair one, and come away.

Why is it that these lines from the "Song of Solomon"
have evoked the spring, over the hundreds of years?

Concrete imagery gives life to language, for any reader.
Children, particularly, depend upon it to help them trans-
late word into meaning. The youngest among them have
loved Beatrix Potter's *The Tale of Peter Rabbit* for many
years, and to be sure, for many reasons. But intrinsic to the

appeal of this book is the fact that Peter can be known by the large brass buttons on his jacket—buttons that can so easily catch on a gooseberry net; he can be heard and felt as he sneezes, "Kertyschoo!" and as he jumps out of the window, upsetting the flowerpots—three of them, to be exact. And the child reader can run with him, knows intimately the very gait, when he hears that Peter goes "lippity—lippity—not very fast." Peter has been made real. His adventure can become the adventure of every child.

Older readers have made the *Odyssey* one of their own classics. They can understand such emotions as the joy of Ulysses when they can see him returning to his land, and in imagination can follow him, and kneel upon the earth as he does:

> As the goddess spoke, the mist that lay on the land scattered, and Odysseus saw that he was indeed in Ithaca, his own country—he knew the harbour and the cave, and the hill Neriton all covered with its forest. And knowing them he knelt down on the ground and kissed the earth of his country.

More recent writers who are finding great favor with children are giving them material that can touch off immediate responsiveness. Laura Ingalls Wilder, for instance, does not forget to include in her descriptions of pioneer life the sounds and smells and tastes that were a part of it. She remembers to tell about the curd that squeaked in the teeth, and the "dishes making little cheerful sounds together," as they were washed and wiped.

Elizabeth Enright, writing in *Thimble Summer* of a little farm girl's trip to the "cold room" to get the milk and butter on a hot day, makes the room and its atmosphere spring up with vividness, out of such simple sensory description as the mention of water cloudy with spilled milk:

> It was still and dim down there. A spigot dripped peacefully into the deep pool of water below, where the milk cans and stone butter crock were sunk. Garnet filled a pitcher with milk and put a square of butter on the plate she had brought. She knelt down and plunged both her arms into the water. It was cloudy with spilled milk but icy cold. She could feel coolness spreading through all her veins and a little shiver ran over her.

In *Mary Poppins Opens the Door*, Pamela Travers brings the little Hyde Park statue, Neleus, to life. She does not attempt to tell the reader, from her vantage point, how happy Neleus is to be alive, but lets the little marble boy show his joy himself, in what he does. To read about him is to see, and be, a child in action, a child who has the delight of life in his feet and hands:

> He curled his little marble toes and stamped on the earth with his marble feet. "Oh, lucky, lucky human beings to be able to do this every day! I've watched you so often, Jane and Michael, and wished I could come and play with you. And now at last my wish has come true. Oh, tell me you're glad to see me!"
> He touched their cheeks with his marble fingers and crowed with joy as he danced around them. Then, before they could utter a word of welcome, he sped like a hare to the edge of the lake and dabbled his hand in the water.

"So—this is what water feels like!" he cried. "So deep and so blue—and as light as air!" . . .

E. B. White, in *Charlotte's Web*, gives children the essence of summer, as they know it, and as all of us used to know it, when we were young enough to poke along through the summer days, tasting what we could taste, touching what we could touch:

> In early summer there are plenty of things for a child to eat and drink and suck and chew. Dandelion stems are full of milk, clover heads are loaded with nectar, the Frigidaire is full of ice-cold drinks. Everywhere you look is life; even the little ball of spit on the weed stalk, if you poke it apart, has a green worm inside it. And on the under side of the leaf of the potato vine are the bright orange eggs of the potato bug.

This kind of immediacy in writing is the gift of those who have kept a fine sensitivity to the impact of the physical world. All of us had this sensitivity when we were children. Most of us have to work to recapture it. One of the best ways is to begin with what amounts to no more than a series of exercises in the recall of personal experience, in simple sensory terms. And if the question is asked, "When do I begin writing for *children?*," the answer is, this is the beginning. Children look for vitality in books, for the human evidence behind the words. When they do not find it in the juvenile stories that are handed to them, then they turn to adult books, where there is vigor and truth and the excitement of style. The history of "children's literature" is the history of the adoption, by children, of books originally written for adults, or by adults who were writing as much to please themselves as their listeners. All along the centuries children have discarded the artificial theme, the empty manner.

For the juvenile writer, in short, there are no exemptions. The art of writing, for him as for any other artist, begins with himself, and his ability to catch hold of the edges of his insight; to discover and make use of his warmth and depth of reach. He has taken one of the first steps when he has begun searching out the dormant sensory impressions he has been carrying about with him.

A B C Exercises

WATER-SKIING

A good way in for us, as we try to dig down to our own perceptions, is to recall some vivid physical experience that snapped at our muscles and stopped our breath. Aquaplaning, for instance. What was it like, in terms of you on that board?

> There I am, grasping the towline not only with my hands but even with my breath. . . .

> I hold on to the rope so tightly I feel as if my shoulders were holding it instead of my fingers. . . .

> My body is as tight as the wood I stand on, but my mind is as loose as the wind. . . .

> Fine sprays of cool water dance upon my face. I wait for them each time. . . . Hello. . . .

> As we curve around, I feel as though I am master of

the ocean—standing above it and putting corners and shaking it up so that after I leave it, it is changed into foam and currents of conflicting rows.

I'm going so fast I've stopped moving. The sea, the sky, the wind, and I are rolling down a buttermilk hill.

COLD

If aquaplaning seems too remote from your own actual experience, try something very personal and immediate, like the sensation of being cold on a winter's day. Explore, make contact with your joints and bones. What is that coldness like?

My legs are cotton, my toes hard icy rocks. . . .

The feeling of distance between me and my toes when I wiggle them warns me I am becoming numb.

When your feet are cold, you feel the bones of your big toe.

FRIGHT

Fright is an emotion that most of us have no difficulty recalling in our own personal terms because it seizes upon our bodies with such an unmistakable hand, twisting and chilling us out of our natural shape:

I'm falling apart. The thoughts in my head are floating in a box of their own. My eyes are seeing what

they choose all by themselves. My body is moving self-
directed where it wants. What can I use to pull me all
together into one person again? Not my fingers, not
my body, not my eyes, they're all alone doing as they
want.

I had to take action to stop the fear that was spread-
ing like lava from my stomach upward and downward.

I lay still on my bed, with that waiting stillness that
holds every muscle alerted. My breathing wanted to
stand at attention too, and it was only by urgent messages from the control center that I was able to force
my lungs to function in the slow tempo of sleep. . . .
My eyelids ached as I held them slitted in a pseudo-
sleep.

Close to the childhood fears of all of us is the memory of
the steps that led to the dark basement. What was it about
these steps that made them so frightening? Think back,
walk down them again, feel the wooden tread against the
sole of the shoe:

Her heart bumping, trying not to breathe, she
started down the stairs. The top ones down to the
landing were all right. They had backs to them, and
the outside door was there. When she got past them
she felt the cold air rush against her ankles where the
backs of the steps were gone, and she felt as if hands
were reaching for her ankles at each step. . . .

AWE, PEACE, FREEDOM, POWER

Words like these are hard to get away from. We use them as thoughtlessly and as commonly as the pennies cluttering up our purses. But there is a way to get beneath them, as a child would.

Let's think of them in the sense of the words we ordinarily grasp at to describe our reactions when we are standing out in a landscape of great expanse. If we are to build up a language that stems from a live body sense, we shall do well to return to the country now and then. In a forest, or a mountain place, the urge to expand bodily is almost inescapable. We run, reach up, stretch ourselves. We want to consume the tree, draw the mountain in. It is not enough to stand and look.

"I had a sense of awe, of freedom, of power," we say, groping to describe what the landscape does to us.

But what is "power" if not this blood-felt surge and reach?

Take an easily imagined situation: You are standing on skis at the top of a snowy slope in vast mountain country. No one else is with you. . . . Now, talk to us of power, awe, peace, freedom:

> I grow tall and taller; to the roots of my hair I grow until my arms are nine miles wide and my throat is a shouting canyon.
>
> The hill looks like a large white sheet of paper that no one has written on. My ski prints are like writing

on it, but I do not feel sure I am allowed to write on it.

My pores opened and the air flowed through my head as if it were cheesecloth.

I felt as though I could walk and walk, not noticing the rises and dips in the ground, walking on the surface of the snow barely leaving an imprint.

Something was growing—alive in me. And was making me bigger than the mountain before me. The womb of the snow expelled me and I was new. Naked and warm.

SENSING THE ATMOSPHERE

Most of us move through the day receiving the impress of the world chiefly through our eyes—though very imperfectly, at that. I ask myself, How is it that for years I failed to notice the miniature technicolor moving pictures in the shining fenders of the parked cars on the street? At best, we walk along, all of us, hacking out of reality our own notched views, like children snipping squares and scallops along a fold of paper.

Yet most of us do use our eyes more than we use our other sense organs. We have for some reason forgotten how to listen. Unless we close our eyes, we do not hear the chord of sound suspended in the air. We do not let our skin surfaces register for us the quality of the atmosphere around us. We breathe a fluid vapor, variously warmed, impurified, clogged, dried, or dampened, yet call it indiscriminately "air." We overlook any but the most obvious odors. Entering a room that has a characteristic odor, most of us can remark, "Oh, yes, this is the odor of the school-room," or the odor of "her apartment, it always smells like this." But of what these odors are compounded, we cannot say. We can only wonder at the sensitive faculties of a writer like James Agee, author of *Let Us Now Praise Famous Men,* who can track down a myriad of components in the odor of a "poor-white Southern country house . . . by which such a house could be identified blindfold in any part of the world."

To exercise the unused senses, think back to an atmosphere that has impinged strongly—whether it is the indoor atmosphere of a room, a subway, a bus, or the outdoor atmosphere of a place well known to you. Try to feel out the ingredients of this atmosphere with more than your eyes. Stand there, listen, breathe, take your sweater off, and feel the air of the place on your bare arms, on your neck, your forehead. . . .

The Atmosphere of a Basement Apartment in Greenwich Village

. . . Let me begin by telling you that in summer, when people came to visit, they exclaimed, "Oh, how wonderfully cool! Like an air-conditioned movie!" We inhabitants remained silent, for we knew what it is to live awake and asleep in an air-conditioned movie. True, when you stepped down from the summer street into our living room, the clinging heat dropped away from you, and the atmosphere poured over your skin and throat like a cool drink. But after a few hours, the dampness made the bones ache and weighed down on your skin. When you woke in the morning, you felt tender and bruised all over from the drafts, as if you had been pounded lightly and steadily all night by the kind of wooden mallet a cook uses to tenderize meat.

Drafts!—after a few months of careful surveying, holding bare arms before doors and cracks, we discovered that the atmosphere was invisibly veined. Where the eye could see nothing, the skin could feel out a complex network of broad drafts, thin darting currents, whiffing breezes, unexpected eddies and calms. The strong broad drafts that rushed silently through the rooms, leaving sore throats and aching backs behind them, could, we discovered, be dammed or diverted through careful engineering of doors, curtains, and furniture. But there always eluded us the smaller streams that darted through even a closed room, raising a cold sweat on your anklebones or an unsweatered flank, and waving your forelock gently on your head as you slept. . . .

A Mountain Place in Summer

The air was heavy with the life in it—the fervid sun heat, the smells of all the growing things, the wild flowers insistently making room for one more and one more when it seemed that not another thing could breathe there on the mountain top of summer. . . .

First Bus Ride, after Illness

She sat with her hands folded in her lap and tried to fight off the fear which had started somewhere deep within her body, and was growing upward, like a thick weed that would strangle her when it reached her throat. There was no air in the bus, and the people were now packed in so tightly that it was like trying to breathe with your face in a pan of dough. . . .

For the writer sitting at the desk, the process of translating experience and ideas into concrete terms is sometimes not so much one of seizing upon the sensory images that come to his mind as it is one of realizing that he can have those images, if he will turn inward and look for them. Shedding the stereotyped, abstract language that we have all come to use takes a certain amount of conscious effort, just as bringing out onto the page the personal record of experience requires a good deal of capacity for spontaneity.

But spontaneity—the free rush of energy, the standing on two feet and the shouting of, Yo ho ho, it is I, I, I!—is what the world warms to, wherever and however it appears.

There will be more to say in later chapters about spontaneity as it affects the content of the writer's stories. There is yet something to be said about it, as it pertains to the vitality of the tool with which the writer shapes his content. Language texture built upon this dynamic source is not only evocative and alive, but inevitably moves with varied pace and rhythm, and carves out form for itself. This relationship is direct and basic in its simplest manifestations, as children themselves will show us, in the following chapters.

And as every storyteller knows, children ask us for rhythm and color and form in story language as insistently as they ask for excitement and suspense. To a child, a story told without a feeling for the form, the design, the movement, the accent that are inherent in its content is only half a story.

CHAPTER II

Rhythm

Rapunzel, Rapunzel,
Let down your golden hair.

Mirror, mirror, on the wall,
Who is fairest of them all?

Ewa-yea, my little owlet!

Refrains like these rise up out of the story residue, when
we search our own childhood memories. Like the lava cores
of ancient volcanoes, they resist destruction.

For young children, the rhythmic refrain of a story epit-
omizes, marks the way. Around it can cling the whole por-
tent and texture of the story.

Today's children, growing up on a new story lore, are accumulating a new set of loved refrains, such as Milne's:

> The more it snows
> > (Tiddely pom),
> The more it goes
> > (Tiddely pom),
> The more it goes
> > (Tiddely pom),
> On snowing.

Or Wanda Gag's:

> Hundreds of cats,
> Thousands of cats,
> Millions and billions and trillions of cats.

Or:

> My dear, my dear,
> Any friend of our friend
> Is welcomed here.

from *May I Bring a Friend?* by Beatrice Schenk de Regniers.

The successful writer for children knows the magic of the rhythmical, repeated refrain. And yet he knows, too, that "rhythm" is more than the metric beat of mnemonic verse. Sometimes he lets rhythm go rocking and cracking through his entire story, to give it pulse and vigor and fun. Robert McCloskey, a favorite of ten-year-olds today for his Centerburg stories, in one tale sets all his characters dancing, to the tune of slap-bat rhythms that jig through every page. The story is danced, sung, stamped, clapped, tapped, from beginning to end.

In Kipling's *Elephant's Child*, the preposterous Bi-Coloured-Python-Rock-Snake flails and scails through the central theme with sentences as long and pompous as his name.

Milne's Pooh Bear fills Pooh Corner with his hums, and even when he is not humming, Tigger is bouncing the words up and down, and the dreary Eeyore is quietly phrasing his woes, in the soft, long-suffering voice of a cloth donkey.

Rhythm, broadly speaking, involves just this—a quality of thought, a quality of movement. Rhythm is a long drone, or a bounce, or a slap-bat dance; it is the easy iambic up-and-down of quiet speech; it is the sharp beat and quickened pace of emotional outburst.

See how we use rhythm, in this sense, in our ordinary speech, daily. I have just written:

in our ordinary speech

This is the "easy iambic up-and-down" of conversation, of exposition. But let a little angry emotion enter in:

"Come in here! What have I told you a hundred times! Get along! Stop that crying! Listen to me, will you?"

The accent falls on the initial breaths, and the words tumble along at a rapid pace. The movement of the lines is dependent upon the emotion, inseparable from it.

We have only to listen to children's own language to understand this concept of organic rhythm.

Quite unaware that she is speaking "poetry," ignorant even of the word "rhythm," a six-year-old chants to herself as she plays a harbor play with her blocks and boats on the floor. She becomes the swaying bell buoy as she speaks. Her words fall into a long slow swing:

Ding, ding, ding, way in the water deep
I hear that bell so far away, ding, ding, ding.
In the deep, deep waters of the ocean,
It tells all different ships
To not go near that bell, ding, ding.
Each day we hear it far away in the distance of the ocean.
Boats go sailing by, but not so near that bell,
For rocks are underneath, you see, and that is why
    we have that bell,
Ding, Ding, Ding.

An entirely different kind of movement is the quick, jerky pace of this mouse poem, dictated by a small group of five-year-old children, as they stood around their cage of white mice, fascinated by the unwonted excitement and darting movements of the mice on that particular day:

Shake shake and nibble nibble,
Wiggle wiggle tail,
Wiggle wiggle nose,
Wiggle wiggle ears,
Down and up and down and up, little feet,
And all around the cage they go,
And nibble up again.

No one had said to them, "Make a poem using a quick, sharp rhythm just like the movements of the mice." Young children could not use and do not need such directions. They are pliant enough to move, even though in subliminal ways—with what they see moving. It would have been almost impossible for them to describe the darting mice in an alien rhythm—for instance, in words that moved along in a slow leisurely tempo, such as: "Today our mice seem to be jumping around the cage, for some reason. They nibble at the top of the cage, and then they run down and nibble at the bottom, wiggling their noses and tails and ears. . . ."

Instead, the children's words shape themselves naturally and easily into the design, the texture, the tempo and accent that suggest the movements of the mice themselves. This is, on a very simple scale, the phenomenon that Whitman was describing in the Preface to *Leaves of Grass*, when he said that "The rhyme and uniformity of perfect poems show the free growth of metrical laws and bud from them as unerringly and loosely as lilacs or roses on a bush, and take shapes as compact as the shapes of chestnuts and oranges and melons and pears. . . ."

One more example. Here is a ten-year-old, throwing aside useless "ands," periods, and structural barriers, to get the rush of the train onto her page:

> Hurry, hurry, scurry, scurry, like a dash, like a flash, crash, bang, slam, hot and a holler, louder, louder as it comes nearer.
>
> Then shsh, chu chu chu, it stops.
> Shsh goes the steam, chu, chu, chu, chu.

True, poems like the "Bell Buoy" and the "Mice" and the "Train" do not appear every time the child opens his mouth to speak. They are usually the expressions of strongly felt experience.

And yet the language of childhood is full of rhythm, as anyone knows who walks along the street in the springtime, among the bouncing balls, and turning ropes:

> My mother
> Your mother
> Live across the way,
> 1617 South Broadway. . . .

This is rhythm in its naked, powerful form of metric regularity of movement. The strong beat of the chant enhances the pleasure of the rhythmical jump and bounce. Or is it the other way around? Language and movement—dance and chant—are inextricably bound, in early childhood. One reinforces the other. Both are measures that heighten. It is only as we grow older that we must be reminded of the functions of rhythm, of dance, of poetry; that we look to definitions to tell us what we practiced when we were young.

Karl Shapiro, speaking of "rime" in the sense of the language of poetry, describes its heightening power lucidly in his *Essay on Rime*:

> In the mathematical sense, rime is a power,
> Prose raised to the numerical exponent
> Of three or six or even *n*, depending
> Upon the propensity of the literature
> At a particular time and on the bent
> Of the particular poet. It is therefore
> A heightening and a measure of intensity.

The heightening, the intensity, the power, are all known to the three-year-old. Words of derision, delight, bombast, scorn, are cast into childhood's universal chant form:

Crybabies are taunted with this refrain, from the coast of Oregon to the hills of Tennessee. No one teaches this power. Children discover for themselves that taunting is raised to the "numerical exponent of three, or six or even *n*," when it can be sung and stamped.

I have heard a child crowd twenty words into this basic pattern—unmanageable, unrhythmical words—but the refrain and its accent provided her with the cloak of derision that she needed:

Tomorrow's my baby brother's birth - day

My   ba - by   broth - er

And we're having a   par - ty

And only Patsy and I are   com - ·ing

Ha   ha   ha   Ha   Ha

With her "Ha, ha ha Ha Ha," she falls into the easy beat, the blend of sound and motion, that is the delight of children from the time they can speak their first words. Indeed, it is through rhythmic repetition, the matching of word to motion, that the young child learns the complexities of language.

A two-and-a-half-year-old speaks this pounding "poem" effortlessly, as she hammers on her pegboard. The pounding gives her the accent and the beat. Word follows hand:

> Bang goes the workman
> Bang goes the workman
> Hammer's going
>
> Bingo, bango,
> Bingo, bango
> BINGO, BANGO.
>
> Bingo, bango,
> Hammer is a hammer,
> Bingo bango
> Bingo bango
> Swing your hammer
>
> Bang with your hammer
> Bang with your hammer
> Bango, bango, bango bang.
>
> Bingo bango
> Hammer with your hammer
> Bingo Bango
> Hammer with your hammer.

Poets who write for children—or who are loved by children, whether or not they are "children's poets"—know that word must follow hand, that the poem must *move*. They know well, too, as Edith Sitwell says in her *A Poet's Notebook*, that "the swiftness of the Horse is not to be found in the Harmony and Proportion of a Sonnet."

Their horses gallop with hoofs pounding out the gallop rhythm as in this nursery rhyme:

> Husky hi, husky hi,
> Here comes Keery galloping by.
> She carries her husband tied in a sack,
> She carries him home on her horse's back.
> Husky hi, husky hi,
> Here comes Keery galloping by!

Vachel Lindsay's potato dancers dance their lines in a jigging rhythm that is irresistible to children:

> "Potatoes were the waiters,
> Potatoes were the waiters,
> Potatoes were the waiters,
> Potatoes were the band,
> Potatoes were the dancers,
>
> Kicking up the sand,
> Kicking up the sand,
> Kicking up the sand,
> Potatoes were the dancers,
> Kicking up the sand.
>
> Their legs were old burnt matches,
> Their legs were old burnt matches,
> Their legs were old burnt matches,
> Their arms were just the same. . . ."

I have seen children dance this poem. They know what the poet meant when he changed his jigging rhythm, and limped into "Their legs were old burnt matches." The children limp likewise, and look down at their legs, and hobble on them as though they were, indeed, straight little sticks of old burned wood.

Of course, every poet is aware of the movement of his lines; creates swiftness, heaviness, or a light tread with the texture of his words. As Karl Shapiro points out, of Milton:

> The speed of falling angels, the travail
> Of Satan laboring upward through Chaos,
> The sweet slow step of Eve in Paradise
> Milton designs by stress and shift of stress
> And always to the count of ten. . . .

The unpracticed ear does not always discern the subtle matching of mood to movement, achieved by the Miltons and others of like stature. Occasionally, however, a poet gives us a playful experiment, so markedly shaping his images through the rhythm intrinsic to them, that even a child can hear and understand. This, after all, is the child's idiom.

Surely no one could fail to see the scuttling mice in these twitching lines of E. E. Cummings:

> hist   whist
> little ghostthings
> tip-toe
> twinkle-toe

little twitchy
witches and tingling
goblins
hob-a-nob   hob-a-nob

little hoppy happy
toad in tweeds
tweeds
little itchy mousies

with scuttling
eyes   rustle and run   and
hidehidehide
whisk
. . .

And in William Carlos Williams' nonstop lines, the
dancers are impelled around and around, from one line to
the next and the next and next, turning, turning:

The Dance

In Breughel's great picture, The Kermess,
the dancers go round, they go round and
around, the squeal and the blare and the
tweedle of bagpipes, a bugle and fiddles
tipping their bellies (round as the thick-
sided glasses whose wash they impound)
their hips and their bellies off balance
to turn them. Kicking and rolling about
the Fair Grounds, swinging their butts, those
shanks must be sound to bear up under such
rollicking measures, prance as they dance
In Breughel's great picture, the Kermess.

The writer for children must be able to delight with his rhythms, whether his medium is verse or prose. He must be like the storyteller, who dramatizes with the cadences, tempos, staccatos, that are inherent in the story content. He must be like the child, who picks up rhythm wherever he finds it and gives it back in gesturing words, for the natural joy of it.

A B C Exercises

Writing with a feeling for rhythm is only a matter of finding your way back to the lively sense of movement that you had when you were four years old.

"But I have never written a poem in my life."

Neither has the four-year-old.

He does not worry over whether or not it is a poem. He is merely finding the tempo, the sounds, that are right for what he wants to say. He is like Winnie-the-Pooh, fitting his thoughts into sizes and shapes: "I could call this place Poohanpiglet Corner if Pooh Corner didn't sound better, which it does, being smaller and more like a corner."

"But how do I know what the right shapes are?"

How does the four-year-old know? He merely concentrates on his object, watches it, moves with it. He becomes the mouse, the bell buoy, the train. The words follow. It is as simple as that.

YOU, MOVING

Since rhythm is movement, begin with movements that you know a good deal about. Begin with yourself moving—

on a sled, on skates, on skis, swimming, running, skipping, walking on high heels, dancing, knitting, rocking a baby. Is the movement long and steady, or one that dips and breaks? Is it pell-mell? Does it topple and stagger, or is it a rounding bounce?

Possibly your words will shape themselves into a prose paragraph, like the one below on skiing. It does not matter that this is prose, or that the results may seem unfinished, imperfect, taken as a whole. The important thing is that the lines coast and make the reader move with their speed:

Skiing

I was floating along at a wonderful speed and I
swooshed to the right and I swooshed to the left then
I flew down the hill with a bounce and a glide and
went faster, yes faster, and crouching I glided, till the
bumps came faster and broke my rhythm—
I had to falter, I had to break it,
I had to stop!
I had to stop!
and slow up and
slow up and
slow up
and finally
come to a
stop, a
stop.

ANYTHING THAT MOVES

Animals move in easily defined ways. The squirrel nibbles like a quick puppet; the seal in the park swims with a long swirl; lizards dart and are gone.

Trace out these movements in the air before you, if it is
a help. (When you were a child, you played the squirrel;
you got down on the rug and stretched out like the seal,
making your whole self smooth and long.)

Lizard

Stop! bright
quiver
slip-slide-slip-slither
sliver
gone.

The Squirrel

Eat it, eat it, eat it!
Eat it, eat it, eat it!
Where's the other?
Where's the other?
Hid it, hid it, hid it,
Where? Where? Where?
In that hole
In that hole
In that hole—there!
Tomorrow, tomorrow, tomorrow
I'll eat it
Eat it
Eat it!

Anything that moves has its way of moving, its rhythm.
The movements of the shoeshine man are practiced and
skillful and snapped off with an easy repetitive twist.
Watch him the next time you go to the shoemaker's. And
watch the butcher, the baker, the candlestick maker. All of
them—even an occasional change maker in a subway coin

booth—have developed their characteristic rhythmic patterns.

Shoeshine

Cr—*ack!* slap!
   Rag-dance rag-dance rag-dance rag-dance
    Polish-olish-olish-olish-olish-olish-olish
Cr—*ack!* slap!
(Rag-dab!)
    Polish-olish-olish-olish-olish-olish-olish

READY-MADE RHYTHM

If you have difficulty reproducing these movements that swoop and dip and crack-slap in their irregular ways, start with a rhythm that is ready-made. Listen to the sound of a gallop, or to a child sawing. Listen to the chugging of a train or the clicking of high heels on the sidewalk. Let your words fall in with the accent, the pace, the rhythm that is inherent in the sound:

Train

Who—whoo
slowly, slowly
push a little, push a little
chug a bit, chug a bit
push a little, chug a bit
push a little, chug a bit
push, chug, push, chug
push, chug, push, chug
steam coming out the stack
steam coming out the stack
steam coming out the stack
train going down the track.

Rhythms in language are, of course, constructed of sounds—vowels and consonants put together in syllables of varying weights and colors and time values. In the next chapter we will look in detail at some of these sound elements, not only because of their bearing on rhythm, but because in and for themselves they are a source of delight to children, whether they take the form of incantation, onomatopoeia, or simply musical sound. It was, I believe, a newcomer to this country who remarked that "cellar door" was the most beautiful word he had heard in our language.

Almost any child would understand this.

CHAPTER III

Sound

The storks have a great many stories, which they tell their little ones, all about the bogs and the marshes. They suit them to their ages and capacity. The youngest ones are quite satisfied with "Kribble krabble," or some such nonsense, but the older ones want something with more meaning in it, or at any rate something about the family.

Thus, in *The Marsh King's Daughter*, Hans Christian Andersen presents the storyteller with a little set of directions which could not be more neatly and succinctly packeted. The simplicity of the recipe for pleasing the youngest ones is a bit misleading, however. "Kribble krabble" may be nonsense, but it is not the kind that can be scribbled like doodling, with a random pencil; it cannot be invented, at will, by the writer who says to himself, "Oh, I had better put in a few clip-clops and quack-quacks to please the children."

Kribble krabble insists upon a legitimate place in the sun; it will not shape itself on the page unless it is summoned by the writer who likes the sound of it himself, who will listen to it as he listens to any of his other words, testing their music, their movement, their color. Kribble krabble must be sung, o-hoed, clucked, laughed into existence. It will have no truck with condescension. For a Joyce or a Sitwell it will take on the texture of poetry itself.

Andersen's own Kribble krabble sparkles through his stories with authentic glitter:

> "Croak! croak! brek-kek-kek!" was all the son could say. . . . The Hen had quite little short legs, and therefore she was called Chickabiddy-shortshanks . . . and the swallows cried, "Quinze-wit! quinze-wit! my husband's come!" . . . and the Reindeer sprang away. Flash! flash! it went high in the air. . . . The street boys sang, "Tsi—Tsi—Tsi—glug-glug!" and the Emperor himself sang it too. . . . Ah, a match might do her good, if she could only draw one from the bundle, and rub it against the wall, and warm her hands at it. She drew one out. R-r-atch! how it sputtered and burned! . . . "Thanks! Thanks!" or "Crick! crack!" said all the furniture. . . .

But not even Andersen, with his "Chickabiddy-shortshanks" and his "Croak! croak! brek-kek-kek!" can match the inventiveness of the small child, who hears the grapefruit juice going "dupple dupple" from the can, the waves

making a "suchsush" against the ship, the rain coming
down in "dlocks."

As the storks knew, we give children Kribble krabble because they speak Kribble krabble, and thrive on it. They
seem to pluck it from the air about them, living as they do
in a world where language comes to their ears as sound, un-
complicated by static visual images, or by elaborate associa-
tive meanings. Indeed, so much of what they hear is meaningless that they have no choice but to listen to the rise
and fall of tones, the shapes of sound, the alliterations and
repetitions. And they do listen. They hear vowel magic
where we would not dream of looking for it. A four-year-
old solemnly chants, as she goes about her play, this match-
less chain of syllables: "A mouse in a blouse of gabardine!
A mouse in a blouse of gabardine!" A five-year-old repeats
to herself, on a walk through the woods with her mother,
"Master Mind . . . Master Mind . . ."

"What does that mean?" the mother asks.

"Oh, nothing. . . ."

Words and sounds are savored in the mouths of children
as though they were lollypops; they are turned, twisted,
smoothed, rounded, toyed with, smacked, sipped: "Herschel, Herschel," murmurs a four-year-old, as his friend
walks by, "Herschel, Hushel, Hush my baby, Hushel, Herschel."

Even a two-year-old knows when she has struck a good
phrase. Never mind what the adults mean when they use
it:

> Yiks, tie my shoe
> Yiks, tie my shoe
> Yiks, tie my shoe
>   and a half!

Names, letters, sounds—to children who cannot read they are all symbols, signs, hinting of the unknown worlds circling their universe. The symbol for color, the symbol for number, the symbol for the word—a four-year-old can combine them in a single incantation, and why not? They turn upon a single axle, a three-rimmed wheel:

Red and yellow and purple and blue
And red and another yellow,
And green and orange and three blacks,
And three pinks, and one pink, and three browns,
And brown three brown,
And white eighteen turquoise,
And three another pink,
And dark navy-blue three,
And eighteen pink threes,
Black pink three,
Two four three,
Six eight nine,
Ten three eight,
Five three Y,
Five Y Z,
A—L—K
A ten three,
Six eight ten,
Eleven twelve thirteen,
Eighteen fourteen fifteen,
Seventeen, sixteen, eighteen.

Incantation is the stuff of childhood. The ritual words of games and ceremonies and celebrations have magic meanings: "Aunty-Over!" "Run, Sheep, Run!" "Allee-allee-oxen-free!" These enigmatic play cries of children resound in the cups of the summer sky, over the little towns of the East, and the towns of the West. Chants, signals, symbols. They absolve, seal, protect. No question why.

The adult, looking back years later, wonders, "Was it really '*ante*-over'? Was it really 'All-ye all-ye outs in free'? What did it mean, 'Heavy heavy hangs over thy head'? Why did we say to the ladybugs, 'Fly away home, your house is on fire, and your children will burn'?"

Children do not ask. They accept what is given to them and carry their magic key rings about with them as naturally as they carry their jackknives and marbles: Open Sesame! April Fool! Finders Keepers! Holders! Starlight, starbright, first star I've seen tonight . . . Eeny Meeny Miney Mo . . . Inty Minty Tippity Fig. . . . As writers know, incantation is the ancestor, or perhaps the remote cousin of Kribble krabble, and it can magnetize a story or a verse for children. Kipling used it, when he sent his Parsee off "in the direction of Orotavi, Amygdala, the Upland Meadows of Anantarivo, and the Marshes of Sonaput." Milne used it too, when he chanted:

> J. J.
> M. M.
> W. G. du P.
> Took great
> c/o his M * * *
> Though he was only 3. . . .

Kribble krabble itself, however, is a matter not so much of magic meaning as of pure fun with sound. Children like to hear it just as they like to listen to the sound of an egg beater whipping up a deep bowl of cream, or the sound of a lawn mower cutting the summer grass. They have taken the nursery rhymes to themselves for the sake of the deedle deedle dumplings, the hickory dickory docks, the muffets and tuffets, the wee willie winkies, simons and piemans— all meaningless, except to the ear.

They are back begging for more from any storyteller who will play with sound with them, even in the simplest way: "And the scissors went snippity snip, snippity snip. . . ."

"Say it again!" they beg. "Say 'snippity snip' again!"

When a writer can give them a combination of sounds like "stick's stuck," they rush to him, from all over the world.

"Rabbit, my stick's stuck. Is your stick stuck, Piglet?"

What is there about "stick's stuck" that makes it so appealing to the ear?

It is partly this: A "stick stuck" is a stuck stick, as a "caught twig" could never be.

The ability to invent authentic Kribble krabble is dependent not only upon an ear that can take pleasure in the acrobatics of sound, but an ear that can hear the letter "k," for instance, break off the movement of a word (make a stick *stick*); an ear that can find a noisy "d" when it needs one for a noisy line; or a run of short "i's" for speed; or long and waly "w" sounds for woe; or "s" for sweetness and a slow pace.

Why do even very young children take to themselves Kenneth Grahame's lines from "Duck's Ditty"?

> Ducks are a-dabbling
> Up-tails all!

It is because the "k" and the "b's" and the wonderful juxtaposition of "p" and "t" in "up-tails" give a broken up, dabbling quality to the movement. There is a jerky motion

in the sound series: duck-dab-up. Of course, the child only
knows that when he says these lines he sees the ducks. The
words, shaping themselves in his mouth, are duck words.

In the same way Eleanor Farjeon has delighted children
with her Mrs. Peck Pigeon, who moves through the words
of the poem with sharp little pecks and quick little steps.
Short vowels and clipped off consonants put Mrs. Pigeon
right on to the page:

> Mrs. Peck Pigeon
> Is picking for bread,
> Bob-bob-bob
> Goes her little round head.
> Tame as a pussy-cat
> In the street,
> Step-step-step
> Go her little red feet.
> With her little red feet
> And her little round head,
> Mrs. Peck Pigeon
> Goes picking for bread.

Children themselves, so practiced in the shaping of
sounds, have a sure instinct for finding vowel and consonant combinations that put the right movement into their
words. Effortlessly the images rise up from the texture of
their language.

Look again at the mouse story of the five-year-olds:

> Shake shake and nibble nibble
> Wiggle wiggle tail
> Wiggle wiggle nose
> Wiggle wiggle ears

And down and up and down and up little feet
And all around the cage they go,
And nibble up again.

Here the rapid mouselike movement is made possible
through words like "nibble," "wiggle," and "little," with
their quick short "i's" and the hard consonants that
bounce the sounds along; "up," too, is a strategic word
here, for bouncing movement.

Listen again to the child who says the choppy sea goes
"wibbly, woobly, dabbly, dubbly, bibbly." These are
choppy syllables. Even our adult mouths cannot fail to feel
a choppy push and peep and pip at our lips as we speak
them. The child produces such a suggestive series of words,
of course, through no conscious knowledge of the properties of i-o-a-u-i when enclosed by "d's" and "b's." The
child's mouth shapes the sounds because the movements of
the waves are felt in her body, as she talks about them.
Idea flows unimpeded into word, through a recording instrument highly sensitive to pace, accent, motion, sound,
color.

Children have no difficulty conveying mood with the
help of sounds that can either glisten on the page or dull
the movement. See how *The Porpoise*, below, is written entirely in a bright major key, whereas the story of the deep
dark coal under the ground rolls out in a long and heavy
minor:

The Porpoise

Age 9

Swish-shsh-shwsh—say the waves!
Co-weak! Co-weak! Screech the gulls!
I leap kersplash!

I glisten! My fins shine in the sunlight!
How splendid is the world!
Splosh! Swish-shwsh-shwsh!

The Coal

Age 9

In the mine, deep deep down under the ground,
where it is all dark and black, and under the heavy
ground above you, all the pitch black coal comes to
keep you warm at home. In the winter especially because it is so cold. And in the summer you don't need
it. And I don't know if the miners have a rest or not.
But in the winter when it is awfully cold, all the
miners go to work again. And they go down, down,
deep, they go down deep under the ground. And they
do their mining again.

Children show us, again and again, that artistry in the
putting together of sounds is not at all dependent upon the
application of a set of rules and techniques. It is dependent, rather, upon a listening ear, attached to a receptive,
lively organism. Children are artists with their language so
much more easily than we are, because they are closer to
the single source, where life is felt as warmth and current,
and emotions have visible form.

A B C Exercises

Because sound elements of language are the fun elements for children, begin with an approach that is purely
one of play with the sounds of words. Make this, first of

all, a *listening* exercise. Listen to all the "vowels" and "consonants" in the radiator; or identify the sound quality of the bullfrog's croak; listen to the hollow clacking of the children's blocks, or to the rushing of the rain on the windows; and if you want to please the children themselves, listen even to the clap and plop of the egg yolks when you stir a cake.

Get the words down, in any form, as they come. If no form that you know of seems right, invent a new one. If no word that you know of seems right, put one together out of the sounds it should have. You are in the child's territory now, where there are no fences to keep you in.

The Radiator

Listen listen soft it whispers soft slow secrets
    shrill whispers
Tattle-tale
Tattle-tale
    Ugly bungling snitcher
Shush shush listen listen listen whisper
    whisper whisper
    SHUSH

Chant of the Lazy Bullfrogs

(Middle Section an Antiphonal Chant in Counterpoint)
(Two Readers Required)

Work!
Work! Work!
Work, you jerk!

Who work? Who work? Who work?
Work? You work! You work! You work!

Where work? Where work? Where work?
Work! In the murk where turtles lurk!

Work, you jerk!
Work! Work!
Work!

Children Block-building
Bang—blang
flat—square—round—ground
high—sky—angle—wrangle
corners pointing, curves swaying
shapes changing, sliding, climbing,
hollow—bare, towers mounting,
mountains towering, mass collapsing
bang—blang!
bang—blang!

Baking
Shlik
   shluk
      shlake
Mother stirs a cake
Butter sugar
Sifting flour
Lemons squeezing
Drizzling sour.
Clicking eggshells
Yolks are plopping
Yellow creamy bubbles dropping . . .
Shlik
   shluk
      shlake

Mother stirs a cake
Brr . . .
Whip the eggwhite stiff . . .
Turning . . . Beating
Jiffy jiff . . .
Stirring . . . stirring . . .
Round and round
Splashing—
    Clapping—
        Flapping sound.
Scrape the bowl
And do not waste
Yummie yummie! What a taste!
Shlik
    shluk . . . goes the spoon
Now we light the oven soon
Watch . . .
Its yellow crust is rising
Sweetest smell—so appetizing!
Shlik
    shluk
        shlake
Finished is the cake!

You may want to explore a little more consciously the
sound properties of vowels and consonants, learn what you
can suggest with "m" in contrast to "s," or with long "e"
in contrast to short "a" and "u." In an exercise like the following, there is, of course, a deliberate effort to suggest the
child settling down to nap, through sound effects appropriate to each stage of restlessness. In the final stanza, not a
single "s" intrudes to disturb the mood of warm, heavy
sleep:

Lullaby at Rest Time

Shush, child, shush.
Such scratching on screen, shuffling on sheet, chafing and
    churning, thrashing and changing,
Hunch under the shawl, shut eyes, child, and shush.

Sleep, sweet, sleep.
Soft stirrings and rustlings, whispers of pussies;
Cease restlessly fussing, lie still, sweet, and sleep.

There, ah, there.
Breath heaving in even hum, wayward head heavy, thumb
    in mouth,
Lie muffled and warm, while I hover over.

Though mood and color in language—major and minor
key, heaviness or lightness—are highly dependent upon the
interplay of vowel and consonant combinations, still one
should not confuse oneself with a labored attempt to write
according to preplanned formulas. It is safe to say that very
few writers build up the texture of their language in this
way. Rather, movement and color are caught hold of
through complete concentration on, and identification
with, the object—that is, through urgency and immediacy—
as well as through attention to the craft.

Consider a child's top—a thing of speed and grace, with
its dancing hum, its motion as light as a humming bird on
the air. Shut your eyes and watch it spin—a top you used to
know, on a floor you used to know. Let it make you hold
your breath; watch it, hear it, follow it to the slowing end.

Then write. Put the top down into words, in its whirring
lightness and speed. You can do it in five minutes. If you

wait longer, you will have lost that humming thing, and
you will find yourself hacking at a potato. Refining and per-
fecting can come later, if you want to make of this more
than an exercise:

The Top

Spree — ee — free — whee — whirl — twirl — furl — hurl
— circle — jerkle —
Spin top flop.

A Metal Top

(Released by a spring, on a very uneven floor)

Ta
  PLING
I'm free ee   see ee   to sing sing ring ring ga ling ga ling . . .
  Oh so
  low into a rutarutarut
Whee   ee   free   ee   see   ee
  ta   HUM   some fun   hum hum tum
  None nn   so fun nn
  None
        so
            fun
      as
  a
Blue
  blue
      sue
Who
  too
      too
          too

SANG
   so   soon nn
BALANG
   too soonn
   too
       soon
          soon
I TANG
and I
bang
   on the floor
free   ee
   no
      more.

Up to this point we have been dealing in a piecemeal fashion with the elements of language, out of the necessities of this kind of material.

When we put our sounding words back into the rhythms of their sentences, and our sentences into their rightful contexts, then we see that our material is falling into forms, or patterns—if, that is, our instinct for pleasing the ear of a child is a sure one.

The pattern of a story is a good part of its appeal, for the youngest listeners. And the shaping of a story into the pattern that is the most effective one for its content, and for the child who is to hear it, is half the art of story writing.

This brings us to one of our core questions: What determines form?

CHAPTER IV

Form

A four-year-old boy stands at the top of the playground slide. To the world beneath he announces:

> You know,
> I'm not a boy,
> I'm not a girl,
> I'm not a lady
> and
> I'm not a man
> I'm not the sky
> and
> I'm not the sand

I'm really
ICE
and
soon
I'll
turn
into
water!

And down he slides!

To the boy, it is a game. To us, watching from the world beneath, it is visible poetry, thought translated into form. Through repetition, contrast, and suspense, we are led to the climax, where the metaphor bursts upon us and leaves us staring in surprise.

Of course, the little boy is only playing—talking about the things he knows, and acting out a new discovery. It is as though he was saying—though it is never said this way—Ha! Ice melting is like me sliding down the slide. I see! This is the world! It has boys in it, and girls, and ladies and men, and a sky up above and sand below—and I, I, though I'm really a boy, can make myself like ICE!

He is investigating the nature of things. Standing there on the top of the slide, he gets his bearings. What he discovers is something to shout about, to celebrate. And because he is only four years old, his thoughts touch singly upon each point he surveys. He cannot gather his observations into a generalization. He must enumerate, contrast, and repeat. "This is not this, or this, or this. It is THAT!" Furthermore, to him, repetition is the natural language of celebration; contrast and suspense are the language of discovery.

Thus, in a spontaneous way, the announcement from the slide shapes itself into a *design*.

The writer can perhaps best spell out for himself the significance of design in writing by studying children's own uses of it, its varieties, its meaning, its power in the hands of the children themselves at various stages in their growth. Here are foreshadowings of the directions he himself may want to move in when he begins to pattern his own stories.

It will be noted at the outset that a good deal of what might be called the natural pattern in young children's language grows, just as the "Ice" poem grew, out of the child's need for—and pleasure in—enumerating, recounting, contrasting, repeating, reviewing, as he gradually pieces together the world that revolves about him.

At age three it may amount to no more than:

> I'm sitting by you
> And you're sitting by me.
> I have a book,
> You have a book,
> We're looking at books together!

Or:

> Today is today,
> Tomorrow is tomorrow.
> Today is Friday,
> Tomorrow is Saturday,
>   and my daddy is going to see me.

When, at four, the child sifts out the facts about his baby brother, through a framework of enumeration and

contrast, it is hard for the adult to resist the label of
"Song."

> He doesn't take milk from a bottle,
> He gets it from his mother.
> He doesn't take it from his daddy,
> He doesn't take it from his grandma,
> His cozy little grandma,
> He does get it from his mother,
> His little cozy mother.

When two or more young children are playing together,
the setting is a natural one for conversations that fall into
patterned forms, as each child seeks to establish ME as distinct from YOU. Indeed, at this early stage the child's self
is at the very center of his thought. His attempts to see
himself in relationship to his world begin at this center, en-
compassing only those things that touch immediately upon
it.

Age 3:

> 1st child: "When I was a baby, my mother sang me
>   to sleep."
> 2nd child: "When *I* was a baby, my sister Barbara
>   sang me to sleep."
> 3rd child: "And when *I* was a baby, my Daddy sang
>   me to sleep, and he rocked me."

Of course, it is a mistake to look at this kind of language
patterning only with the eye of analysis. One must also listen to it with the ear, as the child does, and remember that
to the preschool child, contrast and surprise are ever and al-

ways a game; that enumeration and repetition are his delight; that while he is picking up words from the air, and casting them into patterns, in order to learn his way about, he is really romping under the nutmeg trees:

> Yvonne remarks, at nursery school:
> "My daddy bought me a ring."
> Maria twists the phrase, just for fun:
> "Your mommy bought it."
> Joey joins:
> "Your mommy bought it."
> Jane builds up the chant:
> "Your *Mommy!*"
> All together:
> "*MOMMY!*"
>
> Yvonne tries again:
> "No, my daddy."
> Maria, willing to let the game untwist:
> "Oh, her daddy."
> Joey, falling in:
> "Her daddy."
> Jane:
> "Her *Daddy!*"
> All together, with loud finality:
> "*DADDY!*"

Here, the repetitions are chanted purely for the fun of them. Sometimes, however, even very young children chant them, as poets do, for the necessity. A four-year-old, under the urgency of March, falls into repetitions that swing out upon themselves and give him the breadth he needs. No other language form is available to him to express such expansive feeling:

> Little birds are flying in the sky,
> The birds are all flying,
> The eagles are flying,
> All different birds are flying,
> And trees, and trees and trees,
> Over the mountains,
> And over the mountains,
> And over the mountains,
> Grass is growing around and around,
> And the sky is all around.

As this child grows older, he will pare down and sharpen his repetitions, but if he is a poet he may still have recourse to them for their resilience under the strong beat of emotion. ("Blow, blow, thou winter wind" . . . "Not, I'll not, carrion comfort, Despair, not feast on thee; . . .")

A way of learning, a game, a necessity, a delight. Repetition, enumeration, and contrast are all of these to the youngest children.

Of course, not all of the speech of young children comes tumbling out spontaneously into these poemlike patterns. We have all heard numerous four-year-old "stories" like this narrative account of a trip to the zoo:

> Once upon a time there was a little girl and she went out with her mother and they went in the subway, way up to Bronx Park and they saw the giraffes, and the hippopotamuses, and all the monkeys, and every animal in the world. And they went home again

on the bus, and then when they got home they had
their supper and went to bed.

Yet even here it is clear that the child can give us only a
step-by-step, enumerative recounting. She is hitting the
high lights, one after another, stringing them together with
"ands," giving us a chronological recall of closely linked
events. And note how important, still, are the close-to-self
elements of mother, home, supper, bed, in this chronology!

True, in the following animal story, dictated by a four-
year-old, there is the foreshadowing of *plot*, in the presentation of a problem and its solution. Yet the language style
is closer to enumeration than to generalization; it still
traces out, rather than rounds out. The path is followed, as
Hansel and Gretel followed it, pebble by pebble, all the
way:

> Once there was a little boy and he was walking
> along and a bear came along and followed him, and he
> ran along and he ran and ran and ran and then finally
> the little boy put his hand in the bear's mouth and
> pulled him inside out, and so the little boy walked
> home.

The language style grows in complexity as the child
grows. By age five or six, he has left simple enumeration
behind and can "tell a story" in a variety of ways, drawing
closer and closer to the plot form and constructing patterns
of subtle and intricate design.

Compare the zoo story below, told by a five-year-old,
with the one quoted above. The five-year-old has lifted out
of his trip a few incidents—highly blown up with imagina-

tion!—to handle as the core of his story. No need now to
begin with mother and end with home and bed! And
though repetition is still dear to his heart, it is colored and
varied skillfully with contrast. The boy constructs his story
as he would build a block house, small block here, smaller
block there, both in a delicate balance upon a common
base:

> There were lots of animals at that zoo. You know
> what they did?
> A monkey picked up a pebble and threw it at me
> like this . . .
> A gorilla picked up a stone and threw it at me like
> this . . .
> An elephant picked up a rock and threw it at me
> like this . . .
> A man came along with some popcorn and said to
> the monkey, "Do you like popcorn, monkey?" The
> monkey said, "No."
> He said to the gorilla, "Do you like popcorn, go-
> rilla?" The gorilla said, "No."
> Then he said to the elephant, "Do you like pop-
> corn, elephant?" And the elephant said, "No."
> And then he said to me, "Do you like popcorn, lit-
> tle boy?" and I said, "You bet."

A six-year-old gives us a story simple in design, yet tremendous in import. With this story, we see that the child
has reached a new level in language style. Here, to be sure,
are repetition and contrast. But the contrast element is
merely the framework for a small plot. Here in condensed
form are problem, struggle, resolution; and the pattern,

turning upon the symmetrical three-brother theme, hints
of the ancient folk-tale symbolism:

> Once upon a time there were three pigeons. One
> said, "I'll go to the mountains and eat a lump of peb-
> bles."
> The second one said, "I'll go to the mountain and
> eat a lump of hairpins."
> The third one said, "Oh, dear! I'm the baby, and I
> can't climb a mountain; I can't climb a hill."
> So the brothers opened their bills and carried him
> over the mountains.

This six-year-old is standing on the threshold, looking at
the mountains ahead of her, and already taking her first
flights out to conquer them. Her six-year-oldness holds her
to simplicity and brevity, as she handles a patterned structure, but she will not be held long. As her story clearly
demonstrates, it is only a short step from repetition and
contrast to the posing of a problem—and this means, to the
conception of story as plot.

The stage is set. From the top of the slide the world was
long ago surveyed. The sky is above, the sand below; the
boys and girls, the ladies and men, have been identified as
the dramatis personae. Now, *action!*

Children in their early school years have taken the step
that plunges them into the world of peers. In some respects, they have turned their backs upon home, to mum-
ble secrets with those their own age. (It is not an accident
that in the pigeon fairy tale the rescuers are brothers, not
parents.) The world no longer consists of ME, tiptoeing
through the jungle under the protection of Mother and Fa-

ther. Instead, it is a world where YOU and YOU and YOU have suddenly come with great strides onto the scene, jostling, challenging, measuring, throwing long shadows.

The mountains loom up dangerously, for this ME is really no more than a baby pigeon. Yet there is no question of turning back. The youngest one must learn to do what the oldest ones do. The lumps of pebbles, the lumps of hairpins, are for him, too. But how can he reach them?

How? How? By what means? What road? With whose help? Whose power?

Our school-age child is walking out, on his little bird legs, into the main arena. The problems of interaction with others, the proving of strength, the shaping of values; the hazards, escapes, rescues, symbolic of his needs and emotions; the adventures and far-flung discoveries—these are now his meat.

With his growing powers of synthesis and generalization, he throws off the close-knit webs of language that used to hold him in securely. The stories he tells at seven and eight are impatient with finely linked enumeration and repetitions. Instead, he now leaps into adventure, moves along through dangers and difficulties to the climax, brings his problem to a resolution. Design is still inherent in his story language, but it has become the larger, looser design of the plot form. Children of this age even begin to write (or dictate) their stories in chapters, each one enclosing a small, breath-taking adventure—small, that is, in circumference, but often universal in theme, and boldly perched on the high tent poles of magic, as in this final chapter of the story of Blackie, a cat:

Blackie's Fight

(Age 7)

One day, very early in the morning, Blackie went outside and he heard a clumping, as though it were a giant horse. He ran to find out what it was, and if it was the magic horse, but it was a terrible dragon.

Blackie tried to run, but the dragon's claws held him back—and with his last effort he broke away. He was bleeding and he was red. He ran with his last bit of strength and bounded into the house.

When Mary saw him she began to cry, but she lost no time. She took him to the cat doctor. The cat doctor said, "Tut, tut. He'll be all right in two hours. But if you cry like that he won't be well for sixteen hours." Mary stopped right then and there. She came back in two hours and Blackie was well. And that is the story of Blackie.

Good-by.

This is the age of delight in the preposterous and the hilarious. There is no limit to the imaginative uses of the ridiculous. One seven-year-old begins her long dictated story: "Once upon a time a woman had babies, but what babies they were! Do you know, they were old men. Well, it happened that she was having a birthday party for her children because she had promised all her friends. When she had the birthday party, everyone was so surprised. And one of them said, 'Oh, my gracious,' and fainted. . . ."

An eight-year-old uses a helicopter (Zip) and a "helicoptess" (Marigold) as the heroes of her story, endowing them with human characteristics and carrying them, in

eight chapters, through many of the fundamental experi-
ences of life—courtship, marriage, bringing up a family, as
well as jungle dangers, encounters with outlaws, and heroic
rescues. In the following chapter we see Zip at the height
of his career:

Zip Is a Hero on His Wedding Day

Zip had a wonderful wedding. Do you want me to
tell you about it? Well, Marigold invited all the heli-
coptesses and helicopters in all Florida's islands. They
had a wonderful wedding. They had ice cream, cake,
party hats, favors, and firecrackers. A helicoptess and
helicopter set off two firecrackers. They went off so
hard that they fell in the river. They could not swim,
but Zip could swim. He jumped into the river. He
swam to them and he saved them. Zip was a hero!

To be continued.

In a more lyrical vein, a nine-year-old dictates *The Apple
White Church*. Here a powerful emotion struggles to find
a form for itself. The child ranges into the highly charged
language and symbolism of the Bible, as she thrusts around
for ways to give expression to what must be newly glimpsed
and intensely felt forebodings of change and death. But at
nine there is a healthy return to the everyday business of
living. The matter-of-fact climax of the story—spoken in
the vocabulary of everyday speech—absorbs and resolves
the emotion. Throughout, the form is beautifully shaped
by the content of the feeling.

Of course, the arrangement printed here represents the
adult's attempt to indicate what seemed to be the feeling
tone, as the story progressed. The child indicated only the
chapter divisions and headings.

The Apple White Church
Chapter I.

The cross stands still
On the apple white church
As though the breeze not blowing
While people pass underneath it stand
And swift move going.

The cross stands still
On the apple white church
Nothing but a church
Not a courthouse, not a diamond box
Just a church
That's all
Just a poor white church
That's all.

Chapter II.

The cross on the apple white church bows
The cross bows as to greet the royal lord
'Cause Lord our God on Easter day
   (Has he risen from the dead or
   Has he gone)
Ah, yes, the Lord has risen from the dead
From the evil evil devil
People crowd the church in glee
For the Lord Our Saviour has come free
(Gee—I'm copying like the Bible)
And has cometh to sit on the right hand of
God the Father Almighty

(The cross was sorrow
Have to tell about how he went down to the dead)
The cross on the apple white church stands straight
Tears flow down from its arms
The church is no longer apple white
It's draped in black and purple
While people crowd outside the door in tears
For the Lord our Saviour is among the dead
Why was it he?

Chapter III.

Now just common days come around
Now just common days come around
The cross no longer draped in purple
Now every Sunday people come
Some with sorrows
Some to listen to the preacher
But the cross hears everything
Missing nothing
The cross is getting old after thirty-one years
But he still stands straight
"Ah, soon I will go to the dead too," cried the cross
But I must not be sorrowing
For a new cross will be in my place.

Christmas Eve, no, Christmas

Everybody comes on Christmas day
And celebrates with joyous chants
With gay laughter
When I went to church
The cross was still there
But it's old and shaggy

The church is crowded with people
Three ministers all in a row
But the cross is delighted
He does not know the last
        Christmas is here for him.

The Tearing Down of the Apple White Church

At last some men came in a big truck. They had tools and pickaxes and hammers and drills. First they went to the very top with ladders. They got their pickaxes out and they began to chop on me. Oh but it did hurt. And at last it was down. Poor old me. (I'm supposed to be the cross.) Stone by stone, wall by wall, they took the old church down. The people crowded around to watch the fascinating thing, the work.

(Now I know where they came from.) The destructing company. At last the church was just an old pile of dust. And people went to another church.

And that's the story of the apple white church and its cross.

The writer should not assume, of course, that children's language patterns can provide him with any simple formulas for styling a story. He can use them, however, as rough indicators of the types of story forms that appeal at various stages. And more importantly, the study of them can point up for him the relationship between design in language and the natural stride of the one who is telling the story. It can be seen that at no stage in his language development is the child cramming his story into a preconceived pattern. On the other hand, the story shapes itself, quite without effort, into the patterned structure that reflects his pace at the time, and the pleasures of that pace.

In short, the writer, considering the problems of story form for various ages of children, needs to ask himself where his own delight lies. If he can find a stride that is natural and comfortable, the more chance there is that his story will take the form that is suitable for its content.

The pace of the preschool child, as we have seen, is a slow one. Through enumerations and repetitions, the world is explored, step by step. Nothing is too small to escape notice. The child stops for every grass blade, to feel its sharp edge, to measure its curve up against that of the blades around it.

The writer who pleases the preschool child is the one who enjoys walking down among the grass blades himself; who has retained some of the peculiar sharpness of vision of the four-year-old—the sharpness that focuses on small details and sees them in fresh perspective; he is the one who, though he may always want to tell a *story*, can conceive of suspense and surprise as evolving out of the simplest contrasts. He enjoys the repetitions of language as much as the child enjoys them and takes pleasure in a story design that is as neatly shaped as a child's jackstone. He likes the little knobs that give him something to take hold of; he likes the symmetry. He searches his story content carefully for the repetitions and contrasts that are inherent in it, so that he can use them as his framework.

Every story—whether for the four-year-old or the child of school age—is, in its own way, a drama. The writer creates a stage and moves his characters about on it. But the writer for the youngest children frames his drama on a toy stage, as it were. He takes a small segment of life and throws the spotlight on all of its small goings and comings; we follow his characters, one by one, in all their exits and entrances;

we hear each word that is spoken; the moment-by-moment movements back and forth create the action, the suspense, the design. The miniature drama is complete in one scene. We are not left to assume what might have been spoken, as we are in the dramas for older children; we are not asked to fill in gaps between Acts, from our knowledge of universals; we are not presented with a complexity of scenes set forth upon a revolving stage; we do not leap over inherent repetitions, for the sake of swiftly moving action. Instead, the small scurryings down among the grass blades are revealed, in their minutiae; through a magnifying glass, the scene is blown to life size.

Look at *The Little Red Hen*, a nursery favorite of generations of children. Here the pattern rises up architecturally, out of the repetitions inherent in the action. The Little Red Hen returns to her grain of wheat or the cutting, the grinding, the baking. As she returns, we go with her. These journeyings are not summarized, not disposed of as a single episode in the life of the Little Red Hen.

Likewise we hear, each time, the repeated words of the duck, the cat, the dog: "Not I," "Not I," "Not I." These repetitions build the corners into the skyscraper structure of the story. There is no smoothing over and rounding out of angles, for purposes of moving ahead. The movement of this kind of patterned story, in short, builds up into a design of an all but concrete shape. The child can almost put out his hands and trace its symmetry. It is right for the concrete world he lives in; it is a structure he can understand, and one that he can delight in:

The Little Red Hen

One day the Little Red Hen was scratching in the farmyard when she found a grain of wheat.

"Who will plant this grain of wheat?" said she.

"Not I," said the duck.

"Not I," said the cat.

"Not I," said the dog.

"Very well then," said the Little Red Hen, "I will." And she did.

After some time the wheat grew tall and ripe.

"Who will cut the wheat?" asked the Little Red Hen.

"Not I," said the duck.

"Not I," said the cat.

"Not I," said the dog.

"Very well then," said the Little Red Hen, "I will." And she did.

"Now," she said, "who will take the wheat to the mill to have it ground into flour?"

"Not I," said the duck.

"Not I," said the cat.

"Not I," said the dog.

"Very well then," said the Little Red Hen. "I will." And she did.

When the wheat was ground into flour, she said, "Who will make this flour into bread?"

"Not I," said the duck.

"Not I," said the cat.

"Not I," said the dog.

"Very well then," said the Little Red Hen. "I will." And she did.

Soon she was taking from the oven a lovely loaf of bread.

"Who will eat the bread?" she said.

"I will," said the duck.

"I will," said the cat.

"I will," said the dog.

"Oh, no you won't!" said the Little Red Hen. "I found the grain of wheat. I planted the seed. I cut the ripe grain. I took it to the mill. I baked the bread. I shall eat it myself."

And she did.

It would be possible, of course, to take the content of *The Little Red Hen* and shape it into an entirely different form, one that emphasizes the movement forward, that summarizes and condenses as it moves ahead:

One day the Little Red Hen found a grain of wheat when she was scratching in the farmyard. "Who will plant this wheat?" she called to the duck, the cat, and the dog. Each of them answered, "Not I," so the Little Red Hen planted it herself.

Soon the wheat was ready to cut and take to the mill for grinding. Again, the duck, the cat, and the dog would have nothing to do with it, so the Little Red Hen cut the wheat and took it to the mill herself.

When she came back from the mill with her flour, she asked, "Who will make this flour into bread?" Again, the answer from the duck, the cat, and the dog: "Not I," "Not I," "Not I." So the Little Red Hen baked the bread herself.

When the lovely loaf came from the oven, the Little Red Hen asked, "Who will eat the bread?" The duck, the cat, and the dog were ready at once: "We will!"

"Oh, no you won't," said the Little Red Hen. "I did all the work. I shall eat the bread myself."

And she did.

By and large, this is the storytelling style that adapts itself better to a wide sweep of narrative than to the con-
cisely bounded tale that appeals to the youngest readers.
The writer who feels more at home with the general-
izations and condensations permitted by this style than he
does with the repetitions, enumerations, and refrains of the
symmetrically designed story, should probably address himself to children of the school age, that is, children of
roughly six or seven years and up. With this style, which
permits complexities of plot, leaps in time and space, and
subtle interactions of characters, enter Mary Poppins,
Freddy the pig, Pinocchio, Dr. Dolittle, and other favorites
of the school-age children.

Of course, this is not to say that concrete imagery is any
less important to the vitality of a story for the school-age
child than for the younger children; nor that sound and
rhythm of language are not legitimate components of the
narrative style. Indeed, it is not even to say that there is a
clear boundary line separating the symmetrically patterned
stories from the narrative stories, and dividing children
likewise into two distinct groups—younger ones responding
only to *The Little Red Hen* style; older ones eschewing all
elements of repetitive design.

As a matter of fact, the old nursery favorite, *The Tale of
Peter Rabbit*—still selling well today—is written without a
line of repetition. The story unfolds as a narrative, without
any design except that provided by the action as it rolls up
its dangers and suspense, small episode upon episode, until
at last Peter makes his way to safety. Such a story, built
upon accumulation of dangers, can take a straight narrative
telling, a pace that does not linger too long in the suspense
elements, but moves as rapidly as possible to a resolution.

Conversely, it is quite possible to point to story after

story among the traditional fairy tales—suitable for older children and adults—designed symmetrically around the figure 3, or the figure 7; stories whose form is built upon repeated themes, interlaced, or curved one upon the other.

In Grimm's *The Fisherman's Wife*, for instance, the fisherman returns six times to the shore of the sea, calling each time upon the golden fish for a favor:

> Manye, Manye, Timpie Tee,
> Fishye, Fishye in the sea,
> Ilsebill my wilful wife
> Does not want my way of life.

Each time the request is for something more than was granted before; the second trip to the sea is contingent upon the first, the third upon the second; without the cottage, there would have been no request for the mansion; without the mansion, there would have been no wish to be King, and then Emperor, and Pope, and God. A design rises, like a pyramid, and in the end, a return is made to the beginning. The story is set within a frame.

The symmetrical design of the fairy tales is perhaps not unrelated to their symbolic nature, their origin in folklore, their significance as reflections of a deep-flowing underground stream. Like many other art expressions which are extensions of this stream, they take spontaneous shape in proportions of geometric perfection.

Of course, the symmetry of *The Fisherman's Wife* is scarcely comparable to the symmetry of *The Little Red Hen*. The eight-year-old will read the fairy tale and spurn the nursery story. The repetition in *The Fisherman's Wife* is not an affront to his pace and his span of understanding; it is repetition of a different order, illuminating whole con-

tinents of life; the movement is not confined to a miniature stage.

The criterion of appropriateness of style is not repetition
per se, nor the absence of it. Rather it is, we repeat, a matter of *pace*. The enumerations and repetitions loved by the
youngest children serve as guideposts, as they find their
way about in a world where small details take on the proportions of forest trees. The narrative style, without repetitions, can hold their attention—though it may not equally
delight—if it traces with sufficient specificity a small circle
of events and keeps its suspense within close boundaries.

Older children race past the guideposts and leap over the
small circles, finding them only a hindrance to their stride.
Yet repetitions scaled to their tempo and ability to concep-
tualize are meaningful to them.

The writer needs only to let his form expand with the
complexities of his content.

Beginning writers, in love with patterned story designs
and the rhythmical refrains that sharpen them, sometimes
make the mistake of loading them with content that bulges
out of them and begs for a looser, faster vehicle. The eight-
or nine-year-old will be impatient with story phrases such
as "Jimmy had a bicycle, and every day he rode it up and
down and around and around." If Jimmy is nine, and old
enough for a bicycle, he won't be content with riding it
"up and down and around and around." This is tricycle behavior. The nine-year-old Jimmies are eager to be off down
the street on their bicycles, on the lookout for adventure.

But an even more serious pitfall than this, for the writer
who loves *The Little Red Hen* style, is the danger of creating patterns artificially and capping them down over the
content. This is an exact reversal of what happens, in an ar-
tistically successful story, where the pattern is the *natural
shape* of the content.

The writer for the preschool child needs always to ask himself, "What design does this story take of its own accord, when I trace out its movement?" Where there are repetitions in the action of the characters, as in *The Little Red Hen*, repetition becomes the natural framework for the story; where the action accumulates—as in the folk tale where Chickie Lickie meets Henny Penny, then Henny Penny and Chickie Lickie meet Cocky Locky, and so on— an accumulative language pattern is appropriate.

The form, in many of the outstanding tales for young children, classical or modern, is almost indistinguishable from the content. In Elsa Beskow's *Pelle's New Suit*, for instance, the pattern merely traces the repetitive steps Pelle must take to have his new suit made. From grandmother to grandmother Pelle goes, and to neighbor and mother and tailor. All are willing to help, but all need help from Pelle. The language pattern, based upon the idea, *That I will, my dear, if you will do for me*, is a spelling out of the reciprocal relations that are the heart of the story.

In Virginia Lee Burton's *Katy and the Big Snow*, the action can be plotted almost graphically, and in fact is, in the illustrations accompanying the story. Katy the bulldozer plows away, north, south, east, west, plowing out the snowed-in roads of Geopolis, one after the other. In logical, repetitive sequences, she plows her way to rescues and achievement, to the delight of her child audience.

In Margaret Wise Brown's *Runaway Bunny*, the entire story is developed within the context of the repeated theme of running from, and following after:

"If you run away," said his mother, "I will run after you. For you are my little bunny."

"If you run after me," said the little bunny, "I will

become a fish in a trout stream and I will swim away from you."

"If you become a fish in a trout stream," said his mother . . .

The refrains in patterned stories often present a pitfall for the beginning writer. Too often he interposes them as jingles, solely for the sake of fun with rhythm and sound. But in stories that have become classics, the refrains are usually inherent parts of the story structure, often marking the important turns, or carrying the weight of the action, as in *The Three Little Pigs*:

Little pig, little pig, let me come in.
No, no, by the hair of my chinny-chin-chin.
Then I'll huff and I'll puff and I'll blow your house in.

This refrain is like a key motif in a piece of music, appearing again and again, yet not at the whim of the composer. Rather, a natural development precedes and follows it.

Other stories that might be studied for expert use of refrains to bind the action and carry it forward are Wanda Gag's *Millions of Cats* and Marie Hall Ets's *In the Forest*. In *Millions of Cats*, the refrain appears and reappears throughout the text, in a surprise way, yet always as an integral part of the text. In the picture book *In the Forest*, the refrain is well locked into the story, but not rigidly, and at the very end it appropriately takes a slightly different wording.

It is often a temptation to the beginning writer to push into one story not only all the refrains, but all the contrasts, accumulations, surprises, and suspense that his material suggests, for fear of losing them if he does not use them. This is like handing a child all of his birthday presents at once. In the confusion of many, the single gift is lost.

The writer for the young preschool ages can scarcely pare down his material too much, as he shapes the simple, sharp, clear design that will appeal to these young children.

Consider the simple directness of *The Little Red Hen*. There are no subsidiary patterns. That is, the Little Red Hen does not plant her wheat with a little blue spade, cut it with a little red knife, or carry it to the mill in a little white wheelbarrow. Neither does she leave her dishwashing for the planting, her bedmaking for the cutting, her sweeping for the trip to the mill. The introduction of additional contrasts and repetitions such as these would only muddy the clear-cut design.

And the story is quite complete with its compact ending: "'Oh, no you won't,' said the Little Red Hen. 'I found the grain of wheat. I planted the seed. I cut the ripe grain. I took it to the mill. I baked the bread. I shall eat it myself.' And she did."

We do not need to hear what the duck, the cat, and the dog did as she ate her bread; we do not even want to know what conspiracies they may have dreamed from this point forth. These belong to another story.

Of course, what we are saying here does not apply to stories written for older children. Six- and seven-year-olds can enjoy the interlinked repetitions and embellishments of *The Elephant's Child*—the spanking pattern coupled with the "'satiable curtiosity" pattern, the action buttressed with subsidiary repetitions all along the way, and the whole rounded with the theme of the melon rinds.

For children of nine and ten and older, secondary

themes, woven in and around the main theme, can provide the material for interaction of characters and are almost essential for interest and suspense, as well as for the many-sidedness that will give the story its scope and depth and likeness to life. In *The Great Gilly Hopkins*, by Katherine Paterson, the central problem is located in Gilly's relationship with her new foster mother and her driving aim to find her way back to her own mother whom she hasn't seen in years; but without such secondary characters as seven-year-old William Ernest, the teacher, and the grandmother, the story would be thinned of its full texture and of interactions for Gilly to grow on.

A story shapes itself to fit the child behind or within the book; adapts its pace to his pace, its complexity of pattern and plot to his elastic reach.

But all these considerations of pace and design bring us straight up against considerations of content, which we have dealt with only superficially so far, in order to clarify the bases of form. It is artificial to do so any longer.

Form, as we have said, is but the natural shape of the content. We have pointed out its relationship, in children's own stories, to the child's broadening stride. But we have touched only briefly upon what it is that the child is looking for, what holds his attention. When we turn to such questions as these, we must ask ourselves not so much how we are writing but what, and why. What does a child hope to find in a story? What is meaningful content for the three-year-old? For the six-year-old? The eight-year-old?

In the end we shall find ourselves returning to questions of form and design once more—that is, to the techniques of expertly shaping the content. Without form, the content is lost.

But indeed, without content, the form is lost, and unless

we can strike off a spark at the very core of the story, we shall find ourselves in the plight of the old woman of the nursery tale:

> Fire won't burn stick, stick won't beat dog, dog won't bite pig, pig won't jump over the stile, and I shan't get home tonight. . . .

CHAPTER V

Content

A POINT OF VIEW

"Teacher, I want to tell you a story about spring—spring in the growin' groves. . . ."

A five-year-old, whom I shall call Janie, has tricycled over to the teacher in the sunny schoolyard, on a bright day in early May—the year's first day of summer warmth. Janie is a pensive little girl whose home has been a Florida farm, until this first cold New York winter.

> It was spring in the growin' groves. Those tiny baby animals, you know the ones I mean, 'possums and

woodchucks and like that, were just learnin' how to walk about. The growin' groves was growin' and growin' 'cause the farmer planted his seeds from the top of an old horse. Sometimes it rained and sometimes it didn't, and the growin' groves kept growin'. There was baby leaves too, turnin', and that's the end of the story 'cause I don't want to tell no more.

Janie's story has no plot, no action. Yet Janie is not just reporting, not just communicating a few facts about the coming of spring down in her Florida home. She has something much more important to say. "Teacher, I want to tell you a *story*. . . ."

In the sounding words that she has discovered, she wraps up her homesickness and her responsiveness to the stirrings of spring, and then she is satisfied and tricycles away.

If Janie had been a little older, she might have called her story a poem. But at five, the word "story" is symbol enough. As Janie has used it, it carries the implication of heightened language, charged with feeling. "It was spring in the growin' groves," she begins, and we need no more to tell us that these are Janie's private groves, and not the groves the farmer sees, as he rides through on his old horse.

Janie's story defines for us the concept of "story" as we are using it in this book. Whatever its form, whatever its content, a *story* begins with an emotion. If the emotion is lacking, we are dealing not with a story, not with literature, but with texts, instruction, information. This is not to say that the information book, from Ethel Wright's *Saturday Walk* for the youngest children to *Tugboats Never Sleep*, by Kathryn Lasky for the older children, does not have its important and legitimate place. Nor is it to say that the information book cannot emerge as literature. It does just that, again and again, when the author's springboard is his own excitement in discovery, his own sense of wonder, or involvement, in extending the web of perspective. Any one of us who has recently read Rachel Carson's *The Sea Around Us*, or Sally Carrighar's *One Day on Beetle Rock*, will know in a minute that this is so.

On the young child's level, the Duvoisin and Tresselt picture books on the seasons are examples of books which might be considered in one sense information books, but in another, literature. They do not purport to *tell* the child about the seasons; rather, the child cannot help but sense the color and the metamorphosis, the fragrances of earth and growth, because they are there on the pages, set down out of the authors' own strongly felt response to life.

The Little House, by Virginia Lee Burton, is another book for young children which is scarcely a story in the conventional sense, yet adds up to a good deal more than an information book. The panoramic picture of the growing city, encroaching upon and swallowing up the little country house, not only offers the child a new adult-sized tool for sharpening his perception of the everyday scene, but also invites him to plunge in with us all, who sooner or later must sense the poignancy of impermanence. "Here," the book says, "you are not too young to know that time will come along and nail the boards across the loved door. . . ."

It is the information book geared purely for instruction that is outside the scope of our present discussion—or the information book dressed up to look like a story—with characters and adventures—though its primary aim is still only to present facts. This kind of guise is unfailingly detected by children. They do not resent straightforward instruction. Indeed, they are avid for information, but "story" seems to promise something different, something for which they are also avid, and they are not to be fooled. They know when the story is not there. It is never there when the author only pretends that it is there; when he starts with anything but his own emotional involvement in his material.

As writers, we stoop to children if we underestimate not only their capacity to experience, in their own way, emotions that are common to all of us, but their expectation that a story shall be like a wide field where they may throw themselves into running, for the joy of using their strength.

We need only listen to a five-and-a-half-year-old, talking to herself as she paints at her easel, to be strongly reminded of the scope of the concept of "story" to children:

Once upon a time there was a teen-ager and his name was Jimmy, and he had a girl friend and her name was Mary. He was waiting for his food 'cause he was waiting in the restaurant. And he was very mad. He was waiting 7 hours for his chop suey to come, and so then he got his chop suey after 9 more hours were over. Then it was time for him to go home. So he couldn't have no date with his girl friend. So when he came home it was 12 o'clock and so he went to bed at 1 o'clock. And that day after he woke up everybody was yelling outside. They were saying, "Make way . . . make way, make way . . . for the beautiful princess!" He ran outside to see what all the excitement was. He finally saw that a princess was coming to town so he said, "Princess, will you marry me?" The princess said, "Yes, I'll marry you." So, they got married and lived happily ever after . . . BUT . . . the other

girl friend was very sad and this is a song about the
boy, the princess, and the girl . . .

This is a song of the beautiful princess and
the boy and the other girl.

To never take another girl like the boy friend did.

Keep your own girl.

If she's mean don't take her.

Keep your own girl friend.

That's my lovable, lovable, lovable song.

Out of the trappings of this comic-strip fairy tale
emerges the intimation of a universal theme. The scene is
set uncertainly, somewhere between Chinatown and the
royal highroad, and the characters slip in and out of their
symbolic parts as though in a dream. The child author
seems to be groping her way through material that is almost too difficult for her to handle on the level of logical
reality, but there is no confusion in the underlying emotional reality. With the help of symbols and heightened
language, she flings out a footbridge for herself, to carry her
toward the knowledge of something she has sensed.

Children do not hesitate to walk straight up to emotional experience. They *ask* us for it. Give them no more
than the skeleton of a story of pity or courage or compassion, and they will rush into it with their own emotions, as
the tide rushes in and swirls about the piles beneath the
dock.

It is an interesting experience to turn back to some of
the stories that were landmarks in our own childhood.
"The Fir Tree," by Hans Christian Andersen, for instance.

For how many of us does the very sound of these words stir up a residue of the old emotional response? Yet if we go back to the story now, with the hope of plunging deep into the old poignancy, we will be disappointed. The poignancy is not there. It was in us, who were swelling to receive the knowledge of death, and change, and loss.

Why has the cruel and terrifying story of *Hansel and Gretel* drawn generations of children back to it again and again, if not partially because it invites the full flow of strong emotions—fear and hate and compassion?

How many children have loved the story of *Snow White* primarily because they needed to believe that beauty and goodness could outlive the wickedness of queens, and here was not only symbol of that strength but opportunity to touch and test vicariously the jealous evil powers?

And how many of us, looking back now, wonder what has become of the fairy quality that used to make this story sparkle for us like the snow on a Christmas tree?

Children bring emotions to stories. The author must meet them with emotion. His stories will be charged with meaning for children to the extent that he writes what is meaningful to himself. It is fruitless to stand aside, detachedly contemplating children and their interests and needs, and from that vantage point setting forth to try to please, or worse still, to "help" them.

The author helps children who knows that the province of the child is as wide as the globe itself, and that a part of him is still living in it; who writes his books not "for children," but for and from the child in himself. This is not to say, of course, that close contact with children, in his daily life, may not help him keep in touch with the childlike part of himself.

It can be taken for granted that children look for more

than amusement alone in books, just as we do; that they ask us for stories that give them something to put their teeth into, something to draw strength from. Call it a "moral view," if you will. This is not to be confused with a "moral tag," or preaching, which is as strongly resented by children as we ourselves resent propaganda in literature. The difference is perhaps just this: The writer who preaches at children has removed himself from what he considers their world; the writer who opens up a "moral view" to children stands among them and lifts them up to look through his own windows.

The "moral view" is nothing more nor less than the material of life. Henry James was writing of adult fiction when he expressed this idea, but since there is no qualitative separation between what makes for the greatness of a child's book as opposed to an adult book, we can read our own meanings into his words: "There is, I think, no more nutritive or suggestive truth . . . than that of the perfect dependence of the 'moral' sense of a work of art on the amount of felt life concerned in producing it." And again: "There is one point at which the moral sense and the artistic sense lie very near together; that is in the light of the very obvious truth that the deepest quality of a work of art will always be the quality of the mind of the producer. In proportion as that intelligence is fine will the novel, the picture, the statue partake of the substance of beauty and truth."

In terms of children and their books, this suggests that the moving power of a story, its sustaining and strengthening dynamism, is felt as *contact* takes place, child with writer. It is not a matter of the writer pushing truth and beauty down the throat of the child, or prescribing proper dosages of the same. Rather, the child reaches out and takes the power from the story if it is there, inherent in the potential meaningfulness of its themes, the vitality of its characters, or in ideas that have the power to open up new perceptions.

No one has to teach the child how to stretch his emotions, how to feel with his new feelings. The writer's obligation is only to present him with material that will not fall to pieces when he jumps into it with all of his vigor; material so reflecting the multidimensional fullness of life that the child will be in no danger of finding it too restricted for the purposes he may bring to it.

The current assumption that children are strengthened through stories that present experience thinned of difficulties is open to question.

Or perhaps the question is not so much one of the value of such "therapeutic" stories as it is of the nature of this value. In the jealousy-over-a-new-baby story, for instance, the child reader may indeed identify with a character who is having troubles similar to his own, and there may be comfort in this, and in the glimpse it may give him of the universality of the problem. But it would seem that the active slaying of the dragon is really up to the mother over the shoulder, since in these stories the conflict is usually worked out, or at least allayed, for the child character by his parents, on the basis of new insights they acquire during the course of the story's action. The essential aim of the story is to teach parents something about children's feelings and needs. The result, of course, when teaching slips in, is that *story* slips out, Cinderella disenchanted; and the child is too often left to watch a group of paper-thin players rehearsing their texts.

The tonsil-operation story is another case in point. It may indeed help a child who is going to the hospital, for instance, to become acquainted beforehand, through a "story" written just for this purpose, with the setting and the process, in order that his fear of the unknown may be mitigated. This is arming him with knowledge. Well and good.

But stopping at this point is stopping very short indeed. Why not arm him, also, with that particular kind of strength that flows from a *story?*

It must be granted that no book, of any kind, is going to fortify a child to face difficulties, if his own life experience has not done so. Books do not of themselves act as substitutes for the impact of real people, nor do they have such potency that they can work the strengthening transformations of therapy, unaided.

What they can give children, as literature, is the opportunity to know the "coercive charm" of heightened language and form, and to experience the sense of deepened self—children might call it the good feeling—that comes from involvement with important human emotions.

A child setting forth to the hospital could conceivably be better armed—if books are to be thought of as arming— with a story comparable to the beautiful and moving *Li Lun, Lad of Courage*, by Carolyn Treffinger, than with a battery of written facts about operating rooms, hospital beds, friendly nurses, and ice cream. Here, in Li Lun, is a child hero to identify with, who lives not in a two-dimensional world screened of fears and dread, but in one that leaves him alone on the very peak of difficulty, to find his way home through his courage.

This is not to make a plea for overlooking the power of knowledge, but rather to suggest that knowledge is barren if it does not include knowledge of ourselves, and our human potential.

WHAT ARE CHILDREN LOOKING FOR?

Children ask us for emotional experience in stories, yes. But it is their very propensity for plunging into story themes and stretching them until they are larger than life which makes them also ask us for certain protections. Every storyteller, recounting a tale of little lost creatures, or of cruel stepmothers, or of difficulties too long in the overcoming, may well have heard from the youngest listeners an anxious protest: "Don't tell that story!" The amount, or quality, of pain and fright that children will voluntarily expose themselves to, for emotional sustenance, differs from child to child, of course. The frightening and violent element which may function to provide release for one child may only feed the fears, conscious or unconscious, of another. The writer is in the realm of many unknowns, here, but can perhaps best steer a course for himself by assuming that, by and large, the younger a child, the less is he equipped to handle a raw and unrelieved exposure to painful story themes. *Hansel and Gretel,* that is, will be more acceptable to him, generally speaking, at six or seven than at three or four; and *Pinocchio* more suitable at nine or ten than at six.

Even the youngest children, however, ask for story themes of universal significance. The writer never needs to condescend to them. Even the smallest children are *busy figuring things out,* just as we are. Their problems and discoveries are not ours, but the process, with its attendant difficulties, pleasures, surprises, suspense, is the universal material of life, and the very stuff of story, as well.

As we saw in the last chapter, the simple "contrast" sto-

ries that children chant to themselves at three, as they un-
cover the workings of the surrounding world, develop gradually into full-fledged plot stories with problems, struggle,
and resolution. The common basis, from the very beginning, is the *need to figure something out*, to order the inner
and outer world. Question, discovery, and surprise are almost always present.

It is the figuring-out activity of the child, in both its in-
tellectual and emotional aspects, that can give us a clue to
the nature of the universal themes that have meaning to
him as he grows away from infancy toward adulthood. We
have only to ask ourselves, What does the child concern
himself with, from year to year? *Concern* is our common
matrix.

If we can take a vantage point off in space, as it were, a
little removed from the earth, we can see the process of
growth as a continuum; we can watch the child digging his
way out of the house he was born in, burrowing, overturn-
ing, building, till as a man he carves off mountains and
shoots extensions of himself toward other planets.

He begins his tunneling with his first questions: What is
it? Where does it go? What's in the truck? What makes
the noise out on the street? As soon as he can run about,
he explores his neighborhood. He races to the corners to
watch long trains pass. He learns to count the cars and
soon he knows they travel west, and east. He asks about
the sun; what makes the day, what makes the night, and
who is God, and could men really dig a hole to China?
When he can send his thoughts around the world, he tun-
nels back in time, puts a coonskin on his cap, and reads
about the pioneers. A boy of nine, he leaps through time
and space, from dinosaurs to Mars, and draws the plans of
space ships on his spelling pads.

But drawing takes fine lines, and pens, and compasses, and calculated angles. He must learn to use the tools. "Can I do it?" "Can I do it?" "How?" Even before he learns to speak, this question formulates itself in gesture language, as he struggles with his creeping and his crawling, and his first steps without his mother's hand.

He has shrunk from baby king to little boy, in just a few months' time, and then a life is spent in climbing up again. Renouncing, sparring, saying angry no, and yes, he learns his strength.

"Can I do it?" "Can I do it?" "How?"

He holds to love, balances on laughter. . . .

"Can I go that far alone?"

He makes the turn from home to school, casts off old perspectives, and measures himself, back to back, with others.

He finds the world crisscrossed with a mesh of rules and goals: "My mother says," "My father thinks," "The teacher tells us," "But all the other boys . . ." He writes out GOOD and BAD, at first with crayons, in large, simple strokes, then crosses out and tries again with pen and ink, and secret codes learned from his peers.

He knows, at nine, that no one man alone builds space ships for a hero's trip to Mars. He looks around him for copilots he can trust. . . .

Children, in short, begin almost as soon as they are born to touch the problems, the concerns, the themes, that become the mainstreams of our lives: the extension of perspective and knowledge, with the accompanying search for challenge and change; the building up of skills for mastery and achievement; the pursuit of belief in self, and the finding of direction and support; the winnowing out of independence from dependence, and the learning where to turn for heroes, values, warmth.

Stories that present, either realistically or symbolically, the problems and emotional situations faced by real children in and out of their families, at different stages of their growth; stories of warmth; of the courage and tenacity that lead even the small and weak, or the old and worn-out, to successful achievement; stories of the overcoming of fear and danger; stories that bring new perspectives and discoveries flashing onto the page, with surprise or suspense, or adventurous turns and twists; stories made for laughter and peopled with ourselves, as we are, and as we would like to be—these are essentially what all children are looking for.

The Carrot Seed, by Ruth Krauss, is perhaps to a young three-year-old what *The Great Gilly Hopkins* is to the ten-year-old. Both are stories of fulfillment after a succession of odds and obstacles. *The Carrot Seed*'s story, told largely in pictures, represents perhaps the ultimate simplification of the theme. Yet the test of its universality is that adults themselves do not seem to tire of reading it to their children. The deeply affecting story of *The Great Gilly Hopkins*, with its tough little protagonist at the center, would be highly unsuitable as well as incomprehensible story material for preschoolers. But some of the same kind of heroic charge, in a mild current, sparks the pages of *The Carrot Seed*.

Likewise, the concern with the right and wrong, the good and evil of human behaving, is a universal theme that can be scaled to the understanding of children of all ages. For the nine-year-olds and older, we have the complicated fantasy worlds of *Pinocchio* and Frank Baum's *The Wizard of Oz*, in which the heroes travel through the pages encountering Evil and eventually overcoming with Good; or a story like *The Hundred Dresses,* by Eleanor Estes, which brings the concern with good and evil to a very concrete and realistic distillation, in its posing of the problem of thoughtless cruelty in everyday human relationships. Such stories as these are far too complex for younger children, yet have their counterparts in classics like *The Tale of Peter Rabbit,* or *The Poppy Seed Cakes,* by Margery Clark, where the characters live in a world where *everything does not go right, all of the time,* a world where there are difficulties, problems, dangers. Little Andrewshek, of *The Poppy Seed Cakes,* will probably become one of the most enduring story favorites of children of four, or five, or six, because, like themselves, he does not always remember to do the things he promises and finds himself in mild trouble as a result. Young children can take the trouble element, and they want to take it, when it is presented as it is in this story, balanced and steadied by an understanding and gay Auntie Katushka in the background.

Young children also take very well the world of Pooh Corner, which is inhabited not by a sawdust-stuffed collection of toy animals, but by a thoroughly human ménage, including the crotchety Eeyore, who finally gets a straight talking to for his lonely complaints: "It's your fault, Eeyore. You've never been to see any of us. You just stay here in this one corner of the Forest waiting for the others to come to *you.* Why don't you go to *them* sometimes?"

It is, of course, also the warmth of the Pooh Corner world that endears it to children:

> "Tigger is all right *really*," said Piglet lazily.
> "Of course he is," said Christopher Robin.
> "Everybody is *really*," said Pooh. "That's what *I*

think," said Pooh. "But I don't suppose I'm right," he said.

"Of course you are," said Christopher Robin.

Warmth—of family feeling, parents for children, children for parents, warmth of people toward animals, and toward each other, in any degree and condition—this is the salt of the story world, and any child who is old enough to ask for a story at all looks for it as hopefully as he looks for suspense and surprise—and fortunately is usually able to find it, in the stories that have become, or are rapidly becoming, classics. Warmth is what makes Else Holmelund Minarik's Little Bear stories, for three- and four-year-olds, so comforting. Warmth, as well as perfection of form, accounts for the popularity among preschool children of *Millions of Cats*. Virginia Lee Burton's *Mike Mulligan and His Steam Shovel*, beloved modern favorite of five- and six-year-olds, is, of course, an exciting success story, but what would it be without Mrs. McGillicuddy and her nice hot apple pie presents, and all the interested people of Bangerville and Bopperville and Kipperville and Kopperville? How many of us, when we think back to our old school readers, can recall quite vividly one story that stood out from all others and touched us with its generous feeling—Grimm's *The Elves and the Shoemaker*? Stories of family warmth, from William Steig's *Sylvester and the Magic Pebble* for young children, to *The Moffats*, by Eleanor Estes, and the Laura Ingalls Wilder series on pioneer family life, for older children; stories of good feeling between human beings and animals, from *Play with Me* by Marie Hall Ets, to Lawson's *Rabbit Hill*, and *Mr. Popper's Penguins* by Richard Atwater; such stories have solid uni-

versal appeal, because of the "felt life" unmistakably pervading them.

Also a theme as meaningful to the three-year-old as to
one thirty times his age is the "discovery" theme, the story
that excites because of the new relationships it unfolds, the
new levels of thinking or seeing that it can bring to the
child. A sudden new perspective opened up in a story can
flash from the page like a rocket and can carry with it the
same power to delight. In fact, it is the element of surprise,
and our need for it, which accounts for some of the pleasure all of us take in the plot construction of a story. We
like suspense; we like to guess, to figure out, and finally to
find out; we like to be left in the dark for a time, particularly if the sudden turning on of the light can startle us in
some way. We are born guessers, and answer-hunters.

The ways of bringing discovery or surprise into stories,
for children of all ages, are practically unlimited. There are
no rules and formulas to follow here. The writer has only
to use his own feeling for fun and suspense, and to put out
any nets, traps, lines he can devise, to catch hold of the
new edges of ideas.

A very small new edge, indeed, suffices to delight the
two-year-old. There is perhaps no more successful surprise
story for the very youngest children than H. A. Rey's
Where's My Baby?, a picture book rather than a storybook,
in which the surprise element is provided merely by the de-
vice of the folded page. The child can lift the folded flap
off the picture of the cow, and lo and behold, there is the
cow with her calf! And the mother kangaroo is suddenly
revealed as a kangaroo with a baby in her pocket! And at
the very end, after all of the animal mothers have been discovered with their babies, comes the human mother, at
first alone, then presto! with a brood of children around

her, enjoying the story of *Where's My Baby?* Of course, this story owes its appeal not just to the surprise element, but to the family theme, which is meaningful to young children, and to the warmth and gaiety of the pictures, and to the fact that the animal mothers and babies belong to the familiar world of the very young child. A book similar in format and idea, but disclosing pictures of strange insects or little-known wild beasts, would have none of the appeal of *Where's My Baby?* for very young children.

Another picture-story book that pleases for what might be considered a surprise element, as well as for its pure nonsense, is Ruth Krauss's *Bears*. Here the "new edge" is nothing but the seemingly unlimited number of rhymes for "bears." Those bears keep on appearing, page after page, first on the stairs, then under chairs and washing hairs, and even as millionaires, and finally just "everywheres."

In *The Quiet Noisy Book*, by Margaret Wise Brown, surprise, and the delight of discovery, are present in the plan of the story itself, which is nothing more than a guessing game, carried on in similes, some of them realistic in their concepts, some of them fanciful nonsense, all of them as inviting as surprise packages, waiting on a birthday morning to be broken into. What was the "quiet noise"? Was it a "skyscraper scraping the sky"? A "grasshopper sneezing"? It was a sound "as quiet as someone whispering a secret to a baby. . . ." Part of the fun of such a story is that the child himself can participate. He can measure and weigh the quietness of the noise made by "the flies opening their million-cornered eyes" and think of a quieter noise himself, if he chooses.

Such stories as *Where's My Baby?*, *Bears* and *The Quiet Noisy Book* are without true plot, as are many of the gamelike stories and old nursery tales that appeal to the

youngest children. However, it is possible to write very successful plot stories for children even as young as three, as
the Zemachs' small stories in *The Princess and Froggie*
demonstrate very ably. Even at three, children are in-
trigued by the formula: I'm in trouble—What will I do?—
Now it's all right. These Princess stories have, of course, no
intricacies of development, but manage to sustain suspense
for the brief time that is right for a young child, and to
bring about a satisfying resolution.

Another plot story which delights all preschool children
is Slobodkina's *Caps for Sale*, with its pattern of trouble—
action—resolution. It is, of course, not merely the plot construction of this story which provides the element of surprise, but the particular nature of the answer to the problem. When the monkeys, all in one great gesture, throw
down their caps, aping the man beneath the tree, the child
reader is given, in one sudden flash, a look into meanings
that are probably too obscure for his complete understanding, but for that reason lure him and draw him on in
the attempt to figure them out: Monkeys—apes—to ape is
to copy. . . .

It is likely that a good many children miss this revelation
and simply enjoy the unexpected twist that brings the ped-
dler suddenly out of his dilemma. This story is solidly built
upon surprise, no matter how you look at it—the surprise
of a joke, a game, a trick, a new perspective.

The "new perspective" stories, for children of all ages,
are perhaps among the most numerous of those which
depend upon what I have called the theme of discovery for
their appeal. Many of these are information books, rather
than true stories, but are lifted out of the category of the
factual text by their power to shake up the old proportions
of things and reveal the familiar in a new arrangement. As

we have pointed out before, they convey the author's own feeling for wonder, on the child's penetrating level of seeing. Many of these books deal with the surrounding world of people and work; some are science books; some, for school-age children, handle historical and geographical material.

We have already mentioned *The Little House* as an example of this kind of book; others, for even younger children, are Frances Fox's *The Little Cat Who Could Not Sleep*, which illuminates a corner of the night, revealing to the child reader (and the adult reader, too), the sleeping ways of his daytime animal friends, and Raymond Briggs's wordless picture book, *The Snowman*, in which the wonders of our everyday gadgets are discovered by someone who has never seen them before.

Among the outstanding science books of this nature for children of five or six, two might be mentioned which make a direct attack on the child's perspective, the Schneiders' *How Big is Big?* and Lenore Klein's *Tom and the Small Ant*. In both of these the reader is helped to vividly perceive the relativity of bigness and smallness.

For children of eight or nine, the Schneiders and illustrator Symeon Shimin have produced a magnificent "new perspective" book, *You Among the Stars*. Through the quality of its illustrations, as well as through its actual text, a tremendous sense of universe is conveyed, as the child learns to write the "address of the earth."

As examples of social studies books, whose disclosing of new relationships lifts them out of the realm of purely factual texts for young school-age children, several are particularly illustrative: *The Gulf Stream*, by Ruth Brindze, which with almost the appeal of a detective yarn uncovers for the child the hidden river that flows through the sea;

and the more recent *The Changing City*, by Jörg Müller—
actually a portfolio of pictures rather than a book—
revealing the dramatic changes taking place in a few city
blocks over a period of twenty-three years. Also in this category are Jean Fritz's short biographies of heroes of early
American history—for instance, *Where Was Patrick Henry
on the 29th of May?*—in which she gives new human di-
mensions to the famous and often formidable people
young children meet in their textbooks.

Whatever the theme of a story, its universality and
significance seem dependent upon the use it can make of
the important material of life; and its power to influence
is accomplished not through presentation of carefully
thought-out, exemplary attitudes and lessons, but rather
through the fullness and felt quality of what it reflects.
Children take from books what they need and want to
take; they project themselves into the story's life and find
their own meanings. It is this activity on their part which
starts the wheels of influence turning.

Writers who are grinding axes in their stories run the
danger of presenting such limited, artificial material that
the child will pass it by, unable to find a way in for himself.
He needs a full story world, into which he can plunge and
then move about like a young rabbit, exploring a new
meadow. If there are axes to be ground, he wants to be the
one who does the grinding.

This does not mean, of course, that the writer flings his
child reader down into the midst of an indiscriminate sea
of emotional situations. Children need to be using their capacities for emotional responsiveness, to be sure, but they
can wilt, or harden, in an environment which withholds
warmth, or exposes them to too much fear and violence.

Furthermore, the writer of a story is in the position of the adult who stands before the inquiring, scrutinizing child with his values in his hands. "Show me what the world is like, and what you who have lived here a long time have made of it. . . ." "What can I expect of you?" the child challenges.

It would seem up to us to look closely at the answers we are giving him, embodied in the theme of our stories. How much vicious aggression do we want to stand by? How much belittlement of any group of human beings? How much torment loosed upon a child?

The writer does not preach, does not tag his story with morals, but transmits value through himself; that is, through the quality and reach of his discernment, judgment, and feeling.

THE FANTASY-REALITY QUESTION

Because children of two and three have as yet cleared for themselves only a very small acreage, in terms of grasp of relationships, knowledge of the workings of the world, sense of present and past, far away and near, it seems a foregone conclusion that the writer who hopes to reach them needs to restrict himself to what is clearly understandable to them. Kittens may lose their mittens, in the three-year-old story world, but not princes their kingdoms. Child characters may find their lost pets snuggling in unexpected pockets, but wooden puppets may not locate their fathers surviving in the vast interiors of the whales who have swallowed them. Surprise packages may lie heaped on the pages, but fairy godmothers may not have whisked them down from the empty air, with the touch of a magic wand.

As the child develops gradually a sense of what is real and what is unreal, the writer can venture more and more, along with him, into the realm of the symbolic, the fanciful.

Those educators and psychologists who have wished to take the fairy tale out of the nursery have never made a plea for the literal, nor intended a ban on make-believe for children who were old enough to understand it. Rather, they have seen clearly that the traditional fairy tale of Grimm and Andersen was often far too complex and confusing to have meaning before the ages of seven or eight. Likewise, they have hesitated to present to young children—as adults presenting values—a world structured around themes of extreme cruelty, mutilation, deception. The objection has been not to fantasy per se, but to confusion of time and place, a dubious social code, and the aura of violence.

It would seem that the pertinent question for the writer who is addressing himself to children of approximately four or five and older—that is, children who are old enough to distinguish the real from the unreal—is not *How realistic do I need to be?* or *How fanciful may I become?*, but rather, *What does this story say to the child? What is its theme?*

A child can be shown a threatening world and an over-complicated world through the medium of realism as surely as through fantasy. Those of us who have worked with and observed preschool children with books over a period of years have reason to believe that realistic stories of houses afire or of homeless animals often stir up fears, or expose young children to more anxiety than they are ready to take; that danger-laden pictures, even though illustrative of "realistic" characters—as of the burglar attempting to stab the dog in *Caleb and Kate,* by William Steig, or of the heron about to snap up the tadpole in Marjorie Flack's *Tim Tadpole and the Great Bullfrog*—may seem as threatening to a young child as any pictured giant. Indeed, one wonders whether evils and injustices may not be even more disturbing to the very young child when depicted in real-life terms than when presented in the make-believe and thus somewhat softened form structured by the fairy-tale tradition. However this may be, there seems little ground for singling out and stamping the fantasy story as the only carrier of danger and threat to children in the preschool or early school years.

Conversely, there is no reason to assume that the reality story can best convey gaiety and warmth and human feeling to children during these early years. Surely the antics of H. A. Rey's Curious George, only loosely anchored in reality, have given nothing but pure delight to many a four- or five-year-old; surely the fantastic and beloved *Millions of Cats* carries strong undertones of warmth; and Ruth Krauss's *The Happy Day,* an impossible tale, may well become to children a symbol for the excitement in the discovery of first signs of spring. Among the traditional fairy tales, such stories as Andersen's *The Emperor's New Clothes* and *Snow White* are devoted to the pursuit and praise of what is enduringly good. All of these stories are a far cry from the Bluebeards of fairy-tale lore. The difference is in the substance and tone of the basic themes, not in the use of the make-believe framework.

It has often been assumed that the fantasy story has a corner on imagination and the thrill of adventure. But the well-worn copies of *The Little Auto* and *The Little Air-*

plane by Lois Lenski, and *Mike Mulligan and His Steam Shovel* to be found on nursery and kindergarten shelves are indications that children can find the adventurous aspects of the world of transportation and industrial processes enormously exciting. If the writer has imagination to begin with, it would seem that a real-life setting need not necessarily present barriers to the use of it, nor limit the field for the child reader.

However, a story like *Mike Mulligan and His Steam Shovel* has endeared itself to children not solely for its suspense and excitement, but because the man and his steam shovel are characters the child can easily identify with. As Mike Mulligan and Mary Anne work at full steam to dig the cellar of the new city hall, before the setting of the sun, the child can experience, through them, every challenge he has ever met, every need to prove himself. Their effort and triumph are his.

It is in relation to this symbolic use of stories that it is interesting to speculate whether, by and large, the child can transform steam shovels, tugboats, and other real-life elements into *emotional symbols* as readily as he can unreal giants and witches and fairies. In the giant, or witch, the child has a traditional symbol for fear, or evil; the figure has no other reality to him. His own fear can quickly latch on and get into movement; whereas a real-life runaway horse, or shrieking fire engine—both of which might conceivably be made to function as symbols of fear—may first have to be translated by the child, stripped of some of the trappings of their realistic identity, before he can use them in his own symbolic way.

A certain amount of ambiguity, or distance, seems to facilitate the process of emotional identification. Psychologists have found this true, in their use of projective pic-

ture techniques. The unstructured pictures, those with
hazy outlines and meanings, are the ones that bring out the
richest flow of personal emotional response. (In this con-
nection, one cannot help but question the usefulness of the
technique of pictorial illustration in which the hero is a real
child, photographed in his own home. How easily can the
child reader find himself in this real Billy or Jimmy, who
clearly has curly hair and wears a striped jersey and red
overalls, one strap a little shorter than the other? The too-
literal illustration, like the too-limited, didactic theme, may
thin a story to the point of ineffectualness.)

Though we are suggesting that the ancient and traditional witches, giants, princesses, and cruel stepmothers
have by no means outlived their usefulness, still there
seems little reason to consider them as necessarily timeless,
unchanging emotional symbols, springing from a fixed
source in the deep unconscious of human beings. Possibly
our culture will gradually produce new symbols—if it is not
already doing so, in its quasi-fantastic rocket ships, space
villains, ray guns—that are just as potently charged. These
are for the writer himself to discover.

It is likely that the animal story, in which animals act as
people, will not outgrow its popularity among young children. Animal characters are scarcely ambiguous symbols,
yet they are one step removed from human beings, and for
this reason invite the child to project himself freely into
them. When a bunny is pictured running away, or a puppy
is shown rebelling against the things he should do, the
child can use the distance between them and himself as a
margin of safety, permitting him to experience vicariously
what he might not otherwise feel free to experience.
Identification with animals is phenomenally easy for him,
anyway, as anyone knows who has watched a child turning

himself into a baby kitten or a spirited horse as he plays. The border line between the human baby and the animal baby seems almost nonexistent to the three- or four-year-old, for his play purposes—and that is to say, for his reliving and integrating of experience.

Furthermore, rabbits, bears, and billy goats are without skin color; they do not lose their teeth at six, or freckle in the sun; red hair, blond hair, black hair, are unknown. Any child can slip into their ample fur and play the part.

The fantasy-reality question boils itself down, in the long run, to a matter of the writer's choice. Children, beyond the young preschool years, have their uses for both the real and the unreal story worlds. The writer's concern should be that he follow his own bent; beyond this, the problems that confront him will be the same, whether he peoples his stories with giants or tugboats. That is, he must temper the comprehensibility and complexity of his material to the capacities of the child for whom the story is written, producing neither a fantastic *Pinocchio* nor a realistic *The Great Gilly Hopkins* for the four-year-old; and he must come to terms with his basic themes, recognizing that Bluebeards can appear in any guise, and standing ready to question them and the values and motives they represent, if he finds them in his own stories.

CHAPTER VI

Some Common Pitfalls

FANTASY HAS ITS OWN LOGIC

Anyone who writes fantasy sooner or later discovers its stringent demands. The fantasy story world, in its mechanics, is like a planet off in a distant nebula, moving in its course quite independently of planet earth. The writer must make his choice. If he leaps off to the fantasy planet, he must stay there, making no attempt to keep one foot back in his own world. He may find ways to bring the two worlds startlingly close together, but not so close that the inhabitants may scamper from one to the other, trailing their own planetary insignia behind them.

In short, the writing of fantasy is not a matter of letting the imagination go careening forth, to upset all the delicate canons of the plausible. The fantasy world, like the reality world, has its inner laws; and when the two worlds meet, there must be no tampering with the gyroscopic balance of either one of them.

Take an example: Suppose the writer wants to whisk his child character off on a magic nighttime visit to a make-believe land. This need not pose any problem, for him or for the reader. A dream mechanism here, in this particular instance, probably would not offend the child reader's wish to keep magic inviolate. But even without the dream, the trip to the fantasy world might be made entirely plausible —as it is in *The Wizard of Oz*—if the writer makes the transition at the very outset of the story, without any lingering in the real-life setting. In this way the reader is not allowed to build up a set of images or expectations that will be jolted with the entry of magical creatures. He is given his bearings and his instructions on page one, as it were, and it is up to him from that point forth to gear himself for fantasy.

So far, so good. The only pitfall, in our hypothetical story, is in the return to the real world, which must be made at the end of the adventure to round out the story and leave the hero where the reader found him. This can be very successfully accomplished if the hero wakes up in bed, or simply finds himself at home again. The real world and the fantasy worlds have not actually touched, in any way that stretches the reader's willingness to lend belief. Such a violation would occur, however, if the writer lets the hero bring back with him to the real world a gift from the make-believe land—the magic cape he wore there, or any other tangible token of his trip. Fantasy objects can have no substance in the chemistry of planet earth. This kind of intermingling of two worlds puzzles and dissatisfies the reader. All the logic he knows goes whirling off into the void. An all-or-none system is a requisite.

In those classic stories in which the real and the unreal worlds appear to mingle, I think it will be found in every case that the writer has used some subtle safeguard to keep him from transgressing the laws of logic, or violating the reader's need for consistency.

This is particularly the case in those stories where real people appear to enter the world of talking animals. Milne, for instance, to all intents and purposes, seems to have let a real little boy, Christopher Robin, walk bodily into the imaginary woods where his animated toy animals have their homes. But a second glance will show that this is not so. Christopher Robin is not quite a real child. Milne has given him a tree house in the woods for his home. The reader is thus asked to put a slight film of make-believe around him, which lifts the entire story satisfactorily into the realm of fantasy. Milne never introduces the false note which would be there if Christopher Robin appeared, for even one moment, in a real-life setting, surrounded by the adult members of his family.

Robert Lawson, in *Rabbit Hill*, brings the fantasy and real worlds as close together as it is possible to bring them in a story, without introducing confusion. He shows us the two worlds existing side by side and even occasionally appearing to overlap. His half-human, talking rabbits do cross over from their make-believe world in the garden to the real house, inhabited by a real family. However, when this happens, the real people see the animals only as real rabbits, and the entire relationship between them is ostensibly that of people and animals in the real world. All magic accouterments are left behind, *so far as the real world inhabitants can see.* Of course, this does not keep the rabbits from making their private observations and talking to themselves! The important point here is that the animals are not allowed to talk to the people. The dynamics of the real world's logic are not interfered with, when the locus of the point of view is the real world.

In *The Wind in the Willows*, animals do talk to people, and people to animals. But this preposterous situation is made acceptable just through its preposterousness. The reader accepts the whole world as a symbolic one, as soon as he is aware that "people" encounter these talking, human-size animals in a perfectly matter-of-fact way.

The crux for the writer is just this: When fantasy and reality overlap, the reality world must be put upon a plane one step removed from the actual here and now. A mythical remoteness, or a preposterous matter-of-factness, very obvious pretense, or any symbolic treatment the writer can devise, will allow for the illusion of reality and yet protect the demands of logic.

This bridging of the two worlds, however, does not constitute the whole problem. The inner consistency of fantasy hangs upon the maintaining of a number of delicate adjustments relative to the axis which is the point of departure. Though fantasy can turn upon several axes, if it is allowed to go listing off on more than one at a time in the same story, its persuasiveness will be weakened. Suppose, for example, that the writer is personifying a train, in a story for preschool children. In this personification, the train is endowed with feelings and thoughts, but in its functioning it is a true train, running according to the laws of trains as we know them. Such personification is highly acceptable to young children and need make for no difficulties. Suppose, however, that halfway through the story the train, in a fit of rebellion, blinks off its headlights. The engineer investigates, thinks he has found a mechanical trouble, and turns the lights on again. But the writer insists, in a private aside to the reader, that there really was nothing wrong; our little train was merely showing its temper! A sudden introduction of magical mechanics of this sort is the introduction of a new axis and can only throw the story out of gear. There is nothing against magical mechanics per se, but if they are to propel the train, the reader should be prepared for fantasy on this plane from the beginning. The personification should at no point be restricted by the time-tables, regulations, and mechanical laws associated with the operation of real railroads.

The inner consistency of fantasy must also be maintained by attention to the logic and meaning of its themes. A fantasy story, no less than a reality story, says something to the child reader, presents ideas, feelings, intimations of a point of view. It is essential that the writer explore the implications of his story, before he leaps off with magic hat and wand, to work his spells. The writing of fantasy is not a matter of letting oneself loose with the powers of rampant enchantment in one's hands.

The reader cannot be escaped, peering there through the maze, accepting magic, yes, but always asking the essential "Why?"

Take, for example, a hypothetical fairy story: A little prince wanders off from his castle one day and finds himself in a strange land where all the people have blue hair. As soon as he puts foot upon this land, the spell is upon him, and his own hair turns blue. Alas, he must stay in the land of the blue-haired people; he cannot possibly return to his country where all have hair of gold; it would be too much of a disgrace and he would be laughed at; he is sad that he must leave his home, and his mother and father, but here he must stay. His adventures in the blue-haired land begin at this point. . . .

What does such a theme say to the peering child? A spell is a spell, and we assume raises no questions. But what about the little prince's assumption that he cannot go home if he is "different"? And why is blue hair necessarily so much worse than gold hair? And what kind of mother queen and father king are implied? How is the child reader going to feel about a little prince who is so homeless and outcast as this? Is this the way the writer wants him to feel? Are these the questions the writer is intentionally raising in the child's mind, as an integral part of his theme? If not, he should jump to his toes and realize that such questions are inherent in his material.

In short, no reader leaves his reality world completely behind him when he opens a book of fantasy tales. There can be no escape from the reality of the implications, no escape from a system of meanings that make sense in reality terms, beneath the fanciful symbolic crust.

"BUT IT REALLY WAS THAT WAY"

Reality, for all of its importance as a basic regulator, so far as a story's implications are concerned, can easily become a false guide to the art of story writing, if it is adhered to entirely literally.

A real-life adventure does not necessarily make a good storybook adventure, if all of its details are retained, and all of its characters transported bodily to the pages. "But how can it be," the beginning writer so often exclaims, "that I can't use this material if it really happened this way?" He goes on to point out that the mother of the child involved really *was* that kind of mother, cross and unpleasant; that there really were sixteen cousins visiting the grandfather that summer; that the uncle really was a man who sounded like a book when he talked. . . .

The trouble is just this: A story, particularly an adventure story for school-age children, must move with rapidity; sixteen cousins can only clog the road—if the reader must become acquainted with them all—since they are far too many to emerge as distinct people in the course of a story that will be read in a few hours' time. Likewise, the dictionary speech of the uncle will probably prevent, rather than facilitate, the building up of a live image of a man, in the eyes of a nine-year-old. Young children do not have the patience or ability to wade through paragraphs of pompous, textbook language. A way must be found to present the uncle as the man he is through a shorthand system of excerpts, signs, and symbols, rather than through the literal transcription of what the writer knows is true—assuming, that is, that the story's purposes, and the writer's purposes, are best served by presenting the uncle as the man he really is. Characterization need not, and often should not, rest on a basis of such literal transposition. This is one of the basic principles of any kind of fiction writing.

Take the example of the cross and unpleasant mother. If her crossness and unpleasantness do not have any function in the dynamics that make the characters interact and move through the plot, their use is questionable, particularly if the mother is the only mother figure in the story. Does the writer have any reason for surrounding her with an unpleasant aura and conveying this to the child reader? What does he mean to say to the child about mothers? (For he is saying something in every character he creates.)

In short, if the crossness and unpleasantness are merely incidental, offering nothing for the protagonists to work on, the writer might better invent a mother figure for his story.

Invention is the better part of story construction. For the nine-year-old reader, the writer must whittle out an instrument that will move rapidly and pointedly from the initial posing of the story's problem through the obstacles, adventures, and ups and downs, to the final resolution. This means that he keeps his story free of too many characters—two, three, or four main characters are sufficient; and he watches his words and weeds out those that choke up the story's vitality and impede its tempo.

TEMPO

Tempo—the rate of speed at which the story moves—is such an elusive element that it is often overlooked by the beginning writer. It is, however, basic to the successful communication of the writer's idea.

The best test of the tempo is to read one's manuscript aloud, particularly if it is a story for preschool or young school-age children and hence destined for this kind of reading.

It is not hard to know if one becomes restless during the reading. It is sometimes a little harder to put one's finger on why, and where the remedy lies.

Lagging of the movement is sometimes due to brakes or weights in just those passages which, according to the sense of the story, should be made to move particularly rapidly. An example might be a story for preschool children revolving around guessing, or hunting for surprises. The simple plot takes the child character from one wrong guess to another. Finally, at the end, he knows that the answer, or the surprise, lies at the top of the stairs. He starts up. . . . If the writer, at this point, overloads him with thoughts that must be expressed in print, or with refrains to be sung—all of them taking much longer to read aloud than it takes a child to dash up a flight of stairs—he will be disregarding one of the most important tools that is at his disposal for creating the illusion of reality and carrying his reader with him.

Again, lagging tempo is often the result of lifeless, descriptive writing that fails to convey to the child the sharp, concrete sensory images that arrest him and give him something to take hold of. "Mark threw a quizzical look at Dorothy," tells the eight-year-old nothing about how Mark really looked, what happened to his forehead or his eyes, as he threw that glance.

Children of eight or nine or ten, as we all know, frequently skip over descriptive passages of a story, to give their attention only to the dialogue. This is partly because the writer's descriptive language so often bogs down in ponderous, leisurely words of Latin derivation, or leads the child off into a morass of adjectives, away from the high dry ground of the substantial noun and the lively verb.

Of course, dialogue has its important uses. There is no better way for the story characters to reveal their flavor than through their speech; no more direct way for them to move into the interaction with each other which is essential for the story's plot and meaning. If the writer finds that his chapters are moving heavily, he can examine his long paragraphs, to see if he has overlooked opportunities to let his characters speak; and he can go through his material sentence by sentence, striking out abstractions and unnecessary words and attempting to put into his descriptions the same kind of vitality he puts into dialogue.

Opening paragraphs are particularly important, for the

eight- to ten-year-olds. These children are impatient for the plot to begin; their interest must be captured at once by the promise of adventure to come, of conflict, mystery, suspense, excitement. The writer's problem, of course, is to provide the reader with sufficient orientation as to time and place, and who and what, without introducing information artificially and slowing down the tempo. One of his best exercises will be to study the opening paragraphs of the books that have won the solid approval of this age group—from *Mary Poppins* to *Heidi*. In how many of them does the plot begin with an arrival or a departure? This life situation in itself promises movement, surprise, exploration. Any one of us knows that on a journey we are apt to be singularly aware of the life process as a moment-by-moment movement forward into the unpredictable.

Regulating the tempo, in an adventure story for children of eight or nine and older, usually means keeping it going at a good rapid clip. But for younger children the tempo must be controlled within the limits of younger readers. The popularity of Steig's *Sylvester and the Magic Pebble* is due not solely to its suspense and happy resolution but also to the fact that the suspense is kept *within the limits that are bearable to the young child.* Sylvester is locked in the rock as only three seasons roll by, not six or eight, and he is not involved in any further misadventures before reunion with his family. Furthermore, the pages on which the rock simply waits for time to pass are enlivened by the signs of seasonal change suggested in the brief text and double-spread pictures—leaves falling and grass bending in the autumn; a wolf howling in the snow in winter; flowers appearing in spring.

In that other great favorite for young children, *Where the Wild Things Are,* by Maurice Sendak, it is important to note that Max moves very quickly from his bedroom to the land of the monsters where the story's dramatic scenes take place. Sendak makes this possible by describing the magical journey in short, lyrical lines, usually no more than one or two to a page. And when the monsters carry on their wild rumpus, there are no words at all accompanying the pictures filling these six pages. Any child who may sense a nightmare element here is under no obligation to linger, while others, who revel in the monsters, may stay with them and their rumpus as long as they please. The return home is accomplished just as speedily as the journey out, again through spare text and elimination of all inessentials. Home is the place for Max now; no more monsters needed.

Tempo can prolong suspense or bring the reader quickly to the resolution; tempo can mute or accent the story's flavor. Perhaps no other language element has so much power to make or mar dramatic effect. This is because tempo is essentially the rhythm of the writer's basic idea. It is the natural movement of the story he wants to tell; and of the thought and feeling behind it. The writer who makes the most successful use of it is probably the one whose responsiveness to rhythm in any form is quick and agile; whose use of language, in all its aspects, suggests the lively extension of himself.

We come, in the end, to the point that was our springboard in the beginning. The techniques of writing are mastered not so much through attention to rules as through attention to the motility of our perceptions. Forms and rhythms, images and ideas, take on whatever vitality we have to give to them. The source of both the meaningful theme and the vigorous phrase is in ourselves.

A NOTE ON STYLE

Everyone who writes hopes, of course, to develop what he calls a style of his own, recognizing that style makes the story.

Yet style, in the sense that we have been implicitly referring to it throughout this book, is not an easy thing to come by.

Of course, style of a sort cannot be avoided. Whatever one is at the moment, sitting there at the desk writing, will find its way into the words and make itself known. Condescension, if it is there, will be reflected, or self-flattery, and intent to impress with cleverness, or the desire to reform and improve, as well as the devotion to formulas and fads, and the need to write what others will find acceptable.

Our trouble is in just this fact: What we are comes through, and for most of us what comes through is an attempt to be something other than what we might be, if we could free ourselves from the hold of formulas and the images of approval. "Our" style is to a large extent not our style, but one plucked from the general air, anybody's property.

We have not searched out and brought forward those very aspects of ourselves which would give vitality to our print, in children's eyes. We have hidden away our knack with fun, our ability to make a game out of the most ordinary act, our inventiveness with incantation. We have forgotten to take into account our pleasure in miniature symmetries, in chant and form and rhythm. We have put too far behind us the rituals, the nonsense play, of childhood days.

Likewise we have forgotten the strength of the rush of compassion we knew as children; the readiness to reach for knowledge of death and change and good and evil, and to let ourselves be moved by new griefs. We have forgotten the stirrings we felt when we found ourselves in magical places; the intense delight we took in "growin' groves" where the possums and woodchucks walked about. And it is long since we explored the world in the way that sent us to the top of the slide, at four, to shout our discoveries. Usage has flattened our surprise and closed us up against the quick perceptiveness that could link two worlds: "You know, I'm not a boy . . . I'm really ICE!"

Much of the mediocrity of our style is due to our inability to perceive such likenesses as this between the sliding boy and the melting ice—or to our fear of being thought ridiculous if we do perceive them. We leave the blueberry cobs to the children, and the bridges with their backs that ache, and their fingers that "just touch the other side."

But it is the writer who can leap from form to imagined form, leaving behind the fat and finished shape of adultness, who will charge his words with his own motion. In touch with the magic, the ludicrous, the lovable, he is the one who finds his own style.

Some possess this motility because they never lost it; others can cultivate it. One of the best ways, when all the exercises seem of no avail, is to throw aside one's manuscript and invite a real child to come and listen. In the telling of a story, without reference to the written word, and with all other audience out of mind, we forget the habits that restrict us. The child's presence pulls us slowly down to the level of the preposterous and poignant and gay, where we are at home again with the easy antics of humanity.

To write a story with an individual style is to put into it the live, gesturing person who speaks with all the rhythm of his behavior jostling and coloring his words, and pushing into them the imprint of self.

After
Twenty-five Years

Here we are now, well on our way through the last quarter
of the twentieth century. A great deal has happened in recent decades to change our lives and our literature for
young children. As is always the case, the social scene finds
its reflection in the books written for children as well as
those written for adults. A thorough study of those children's books that have found their way into print in the
last few years could reveal a good deal about the temper of
the times.

Around the globe we have had the uprisings of the Third
World peoples to reach for their independence and their
rights, and in our own country the Civil Rights movement,

with the impetus it gave for greater recognition of the dignity and the claims of all our minorities—now including the handicapped—and of women as one of the unfairly treated human groups. The "Women's Lib" and Equal Rights movements have burgeoned. And as the position of women has shifted a little, so has the picture of family life. This is the era of more flexibility in sexual mores, less stability in marriage, more experimentation in styles of living on the part of both men and women. This means, of course, a different way of life for children, too. With a rising divorce rate and many more mothers at work, larger proportions of young children spend the greater part of their days in nursery schools or day care centers.

And as the bonds of the old family structures have loosened, in a society already shaken by an unwanted war and escalating economic problems, people have sought new comforts and ties. Encounter groups have sprung up, and psychotherapy groups under a myriad of names, though all with a common goal of helping the participants know themselves, open themselves, and reach out to others. The influence of Freud is pervasive, and at the same time Yoga, Zen, and Transcendental Meditation have drawn great numbers of followers.

Meanwhile the earth we live on and the atmosphere protecting us are sending out danger signals. Conservation and ecology have become major concerns as we find ourselves using up our resources, defoliating and poisoning our planet. Is there enough for all of us here? Is there room? In answer, wars erupt and threaten to erupt around the world. Clearly, in both our inner and outer lives we individuals of the late twentieth century have our serious problems—though at the same time we have sent men to walk on the

moon and are regularly launching rockets out into space on
dazzling voyages of discovery.

And is all of this reflected in young children's literature?
Yes, of course—though whether the word "literature"
should be used to characterize all the books that appear is
open to question. Many are "information books" aiming at
nothing more than usefulness, and others are crippled by
didacticism.

How, then, is the writer for young children to approach
these problems, or some of them, if at all? Certainly not by
thinking at the outset that a manuscript free of the old
stereotypes and dealing with one of the important trends—
the rights of blacks or Puerto Ricans or Native Americans
or women; the frank look at situations that hurt us: divorce, separation, death, or war; the free and full expression
of feeling; the ecological dilemmas—is sure to please a publisher. Starting with an aim to "fit the trend" is starting
with the wrong conception, if one hopes to write a story
that will move the reader and will live beyond a day. Such
stories always must start with oneself, with a conviction
centered in one's own being, with a theme or an emotion
so felt that it cannot be denied.

Let's look at a book that has been with us since 1955 and
is likely to remain available and loved for many more years
—*Crow Boy* by Taro Yashima, appropriate for children of
about five to nine or ten. In one sense it could be considered one of the "trend" books, dealing as it does with the
plight in school of a little boy who is "different." That it
has a message is certainly true. But consider the "felt life"
pervading it: Chibi, the different, solitary one, walking to
the Japanese village school every day from his far home,
emerges as someone we all know. We have all been Chibi,
at times in our lives, afraid, withdrawing, yet steadily man-

aging to keep going; we have all shamefully teased and tor-
mented Chibi, at times in our lives. Yet in the end we
glimpse our shallowness and come to admire this self-con-
tained little boy who could explore the world in his own
way and even learn the language of crows. (Don't we all
have this secret wish—to communicate in some fashion
with the other creatures of this earth?) So the book becomes for us a story of many layers. We construct them as
we ponder the meanings, and they reveal themselves to us
as we return and return to the story. This is the richness we
ask for when we read. Instead of a message about discrim-
ination we find here emotion and a person created, we feel
sure, out of the author's own experience of life.

Black children in our own society are also finding their
way into picture books of great distinction, when the author's aim is not to instruct or preach, but to reveal the
universal ways of childhood, the common humanity. Ezra
Jack Keats, with his shining collages and oils, has placed
Peter and his friends in a world of glowing colors where the
small problems and triumphs of childhood are enacted.
Everett Anderson, too—a black child but also a universal
child, fatherless—has greatly endeared himself to young
children by trying to sort out in each succeeding story what
life is bringing to him. Of course, here we have a writer,
Lucille Clifton, who in her writing style is using a clear
voice of her own. Her stories about Everett are small con-
versational poems, seeming to flow onto the page effortlessly, as the graceful illustrations of Ann Grifalconi also
flow. Lucky the writer who can discover, as Mrs. Clifton
has, a way of putting an authentic speaking voice into
print. Is it a matter just of talent, or of a good deal of
travail and trial also?

John Steptoe is another writer—also an illustrator—who

can write in a language that is natural to him, and can create black characters who live on his pages in illustrations of stunning color and line. Some of his characters belong strictly to Harlem, and can give black readers a sense of pride in finding themselves on the pages of a beautiful book. Others, as in the popular *Stevie,* have something to say to all children about feelings held in common—in this case feelings of rivalry, jealousy, trespass.

Two other successful writers should be mentioned here before we move on to one of the other trends. Let me only suggest that Phyllis Hoffman might well be studied for what she has done in *Steffie and Me,* about a black and a white girl who are friends; and Ruth Sonneborn for her *Friday Night Is Papa Night,* about a Puerto Rican family in a large city. In both these picture books the authors have given us characters who let us recognize ourselves as we are in some of our home-and-family ways—private, funny, lovable.

What we are stressing here is a writer's obligation to create—out of his own need—people we can care about, people whose personalities and problems draw us into that human landscape where we all cry and laugh and love. We will find our messages and morals there ourselves, without any trouble. "We," I say, meaning we adults who read aloud to children plus the children themselves for whom the stories are ostensibly written. There should be no rigid separation. Many of us who are well along in years have been moved by *Crow Boy* and *Friday Night Is Papa Night,* and this is as it should be. The author who puts himself, or the child in himself, into a story written for children will inevitably reach that listening adult at the other end. For all of us, though grown, still hope and wait, childlike, to hear those words that will touch us.

What can be said now to the writer who feels an urge to write something for those many children of separated parents, children who are dividing their time today between two homes? How much of the pain can be dealt with, for young children, and in what way? How can a story on this theme help a grieving youngster, if at all?

Marcia Newfield, in *A Book for Jodan*, for ages about eight to ten, succeeds as few others do in meeting the pain head on yet offering some catharsis. Here the reader plunges right into the distress. There is no condescension. The difference, in this book, is that the reader is drawn into the father's pain, not only into his love and caring that are steadfastly there in spite of the separation. We are allowed to see how he shares with Jodan, in the book he makes for her, thoughts that he himself is holding to for courage in accepting change. So we live with this father and child and suffer with them, and struggle with them toward confidence in what the future may bring. We come to know them—particularly the father—at a depth below the surface level that is so often offered to young children. The book holds no simple resolution, but it cannot be read without a feeling of expansion and comfort—thanks to an author who followed no set formula in writing it.

Or consider another topical theme—the problem of old age today. A number of books for children are appearing on the subject of grandparents who can no longer live alone and must go either to nursing homes or to the homes of their sons and daughters, where they feel they are not really wanted. Outstanding among them all is Sharon Bell Mathis's *The Hundred Penny Box*, for a wide age range, beginning as young as six or seven. I am classifying it here as a book about "old age," but its distinction lies in the fact that it really holds several interwoven themes. In this

short slice of life we glimpse the affectionate relationship
between a little black boy, Michael, and his hundred-year-
old great-great-aunt Dew, shrunken with age but still liking
to sing her "long song" and play the counting-the-pennies
game with Michael. Also there is the in-law friction: John
has brought his great-aunt into his small home because he
loves her for the way she cared for him when he had no
one; but for his wife, Ruth, it is not easy. And there are the
precious hundred pennies, one for each year of her life,
kept in the big old box Aunt Dew clings to, loved by the
little boy as well as by the aunt. Will Michael succeed in
hiding the box away from his mother, to save it for Aunt
Dew? We don't find out and we don't need to. It is
enough to hear these very real human beings talk their way
through this small story in the natural, flowing, family-talk
cadences of black people. When we are given such a con-
stellation of characters and an individual as unique and yet
as believable as Aunt Dew, breathing with hundred-year-
old life, we have a book that will be with us for a long
time.

And what is there to suggest to the "feminist" writer
who cares most of all about writing stories that will encour-
age young readers who are girls to stand up and be counted
and show their strengths? First of all, let me point out that
strong females have been with us in literature at least since
the Little Red Hen, and since Gretel grew brave enough to
shove the witch into the oven. And think of some of the
more recent girl characters known and admired for their
strengths: Dorothy, who made her way successfully to the
Emerald City with those odd companions everyone now
has come to love; Fern, who cried out against her father
and saved the life of the little pig, Wilbur; Ramona, who
could stir up a cyclone around Henry Huggins any day;

M. B. Goffstein's Goldie the Dollmaker, who learned to trust her own opinions and lived happily by herself carving her dolls; and of course Alice, bewildered among the monstrous creatures of Carroll's dream tale, but honest and gracious, and in the end sufficiently goaded by righteous fury to slam down the whole pack of cards. All of these girl characters exist for us not in isolation as symbols of feminine power, but as people firmly embedded in stories where they live and grow. This is the key. Whatever the theme—and we might add Death, Birth, Adoption, Fathering, and Sibling Rivalry to those already discussed—a story, layered enough so that we ourselves can live in it and grow with the characters, seems essential.

There is still another important trend in children's literature today—a trend of an entirely different kind. In 1964 Maurice Sendak's *Where the Wild Things Are* won the Caldecott Medal as the most distinguished picture book of the year for young children. It signaled something new. Max's trip to the wild things was an inner journey. He went not just to a make-believe land where monsters lived, but to that dreamed-up secret haven or hiding place where he could let out his anger against his mother and build up his own image again. A number of other inward journeys, invented by other authors, have followed this one of Max's, none of them as successful in the eyes of readers, perhaps because many simply offer outpourings of feelings of madness, badness, gladness, or whatever, without Sendak's magical touch of story and imagination. But we have certainly entered an era of the inward look, in every sense of the word. Bettelheim, in his *Uses of Enchantment,* has turned the attention of all of us to the psychological importance to children of those fairy tales embodying symbolic journeys toward maturity; and Judy Blume is giving older

readers—nine or ten to twelve—a stream of first-person con-
fessional books that are being devoured all across the country. Some of the excitement found in her books comes, of
course, from the fact that she dares to openly describe such
erstwhile private matters as first menstruation and develop-
ing breasts (children run to the libraries to seek out just
those pages) but also she appeals because her characters
talk freely—no matter how glibly—about all sorts of feelings children can recognize relative to parents, classmates,
and themselves.

Is there anything comparable to Judy Blume in books
for children younger than nine or ten? One possible candi-
date comes to mind that has had great appeal for children
of about four to seven—Judith Viorst's *Alexander and the
Terrible, Horrible, No Good, Very Bad Day*. There are no
racy revelations here, but the story is a first-person diatribe
against all the miserable things that happen to a boy in the
course of one day to disappoint him and make him jealous
and angry. The book has taken hold not only because
readers can identify with Alexander's feelings, but because
the illustrations are a humorous delight, and because
there's a thread of a story building up throughout, peopled
not only with Alexander but with his brothers and classmates, and a mother who has a word of wisdom for him in
the end—only a word, to be sure, and not one that erases
the terrible day, but one that may help him put up with
other bad days that are sure to come along.

Alexander, of course, lives in the real world, not in a
symbolic fairy tale world. We might ask, do fantasy tales of
ogres, monsters, witches, or dragons have value for very
young children in today's inner-life story world? We asked
this question earlier in this book, and in spite of the pas-
sage of years, the answer remains the same. Misreading

Bettelheim, many parents have recently been offering the Grimm fairy tales to their preschoolers. Surely a great many of these stories should be put aside until the young listener has developed enough ego strength to tolerate and profit from a story of parents who desert their children, for instance, or stepparents who deal out only cruelty. We know that even *Where the Wild Things Are* can be unsettling, misunderstood, or frightening to children too young for it—children who are not ready yet to take independent steps away from home into dangers. The writer who is attracted to the writing of fantasy stories that resemble fairy tales can have free rein with children of about six and up but should stay within a smaller, safer arena for the youngest ones. Marie Hall Ets's *In the Forest* might be called the perfect "fairy tale" for the three-year-old. It offers a mysterious forest and wild animals—but these creatures are made by the little boy in the story so tame and gentle that they can join in a parade with him through the forest. This is a first tentative approach—a safe enough one —to wild creatures and the fears or angers they can symbolize.

What has happened in recent years to people the old fairy tale world with new protagonists—robots instead of giants, spacemen instead of brave young woodcutters, inhabitants of other planets instead of goblins and witches? A great deal has happened for children of ten or eleven and up. We have the stories of John Christopher, Jean Karl, Alexander Key, Patricia Wrightson, Eleanor Cameron, Madeleine L'Engle, and many others—all really beyond the scope of my discussions here. What we are concerned with is the question: Are there new science-fiction fairy tale worlds for children of about five or six to nine? Unfortunately, very few. A fine beginning has been made in *Alice* by the Russian writer Bulychev, translated by Mirra Ginsburg. Here we have six short twenty-first century adventures of a small girl who makes a discovery on Mars, takes a trip back in time, and finds in a field near her home some space visitors who are only inches high. Also there is *Bobby and Boo: The Little Spaceman* by B. Wiseman, an easy reader strictly for the fives to sevens, a book of little distinction in its format but outstanding for its point of view. In this story a little space visitor who drops down in Bobby's backyard is shown not as a monster enemy, but as another boylike creature with astounding sensory and muscular abilities quite unlike Bobby's. He can make his nose into a baseball bat, his hand into a glove, and can reach out any distance for what he wants. The story stretches perceptions and encourages imaginative thinking about space worlds. Perhaps in the next ten years many more inventive writers will take this leap, creating for young children surprising new planetary possibilities, as C. S. Lewis has done for adults in his *Out of the Silent Planet.*

Among the handful of other science fiction stories and picture books for children in the young primary years, Bill Peet's *The Wump World* should be mentioned, because it deals not only with outer space creatures but with our own planetary problem of pollution. As writers approach these current ecological issues they have some difficulty keeping themselves from falling into what might be called tract writing. Peet uses an almost cartoon technique of illustration, which aids him in making his story attractive to readers.

Ecology writers may be on surer ground if they limit themselves to nonfiction, staying with the effort to show children some of the interrelationships between living creatures and the earth they depend on for their existence. This can be done in picture books that are not only informative but moving and beautiful, as Alvin Tresselt has shown us in his *Beaver Pond*, illustrated by Roger Duvoisin, and *The Dead Tree*, with its magnificent pictures by Charles Robinson. The life cycle of a great tree as Tresselt reveals it—through its growth, death, and decay to the harboring of the new life finding sustenance in it—is a process that stirs respect and wonder. And Tresselt has found a poetic prose for his story that matches the profundity of the subject. Children as young as five have been known to listen to the reading of this book with unusually serious interest, even though not quite grasping all of its import.

This leads us again to the matter of style. Twenty-five years ago I brought this book to an end with "A Note on Style." Today I find myself arriving at the same home base. For we can talk and talk about the quests and adventures that appeal to children; about living characterizations and emotional journeys, inner and outer. But always the starting point for authors who "want to write" is a good grasp of themselves and their own perceptions, and an ability to reflect these, simply and honestly, in the words they use. "Style" emerges from this beginning.

Arnold Lobel is one of today's author-illustrators who has few competitors for popularity with young children. This is partly because he writes—and draws—in his own distinct way. In his Frog and Toad books, for instance, he reveals those "easy antics of humanity"—to quote myself—that give his stories an undeniably Lobel flavor. The antics are permeated with the gentleness and love Lobel knows young children are looking for, and his straightforward, well-tempered sentences, simple though they are, easily carry the Lobel touch in their flow.

William Steig, too, has a style of his own. He puts a

good deal of himself, without condescension, into his stories for young children. Consider *Amos & Boris*, about the friendship between a mouse and a whale—one of this author's most loved books. Steig is really giving children his own view of the "phosphorescent sea" and the "immense starry sky" as he describes the little mouse Amos lying on his boat deck and marveling at the vast universe around and above. How often does a young child encounter this in a story? Or encounter that other fascinating adult vocabulary of words related to boating: such words as compass, sextant, telescope, navigation? Steig is pulling children up to his own level here, and not only in the words he uses but also in the story he is telling—a story of enterprise, dangers, rescues, two incongruous friends who help each other, and the inevitability of parting. In fact, the book is so rich in vitality and in identification possibilities for young children that I venture to say many readers find in it even more satisfactions than Steig realized he was giving them. For here, in this story of an abundant ocean world and the two who met there, they can reach for and discover their own meanings. This is what can happen when an author writes what he cares most about, and in a way he cares about, pushing into his words—I say it once again—the "imprint of self."

BIBLIOGRAPHY

Books and poems referred to in the text are listed here and, where appropriate, supplementary suggestions are included.

INTRODUCTION. PRIMER LESSON

Grahame, Kenneth. *The Wind in the Willows*; illus. by Ernest H. Shepard. New York: Scribner, 1908, pages 2, 3.

Kipling, Rudyard. "The Elephant's Child," in *Just So Stories*; illus. by the author and J. M. Gleeson. Garden City, N.Y.: Doubleday, 1912, pages 63, 65.

Piper, Watty. *The Little Engine That Could*; illus. by George and Doris Hauman. New York: Platt & Munk, 1976.

CHAPTER I. THE LANGUAGE OF SENSORY PERCEPTION

ADULT REFERENCES

Agee, James, and Evans, Walker. *Let Us Now Praise Famous Men*. Boston: Houghton Mifflin, 1960.

Danz, Louis. *Personal Revolution and Picasso*. New York: Haskell House, 1974.

CHILDREN'S BOOKS

Colum, Padraic. *The Children's Homer: Adventures of Odysseus and the Tale of Troy*; illus. by Willy Pogany. New York: Macmillan, 1962, page 18.

Enright, Elizabeth. *Thimble Summer*; illus. by the author. New York: Holt, Rinehart & Winston, 1966, page 9.

Potter, Beatrix. *The Tale of Peter Rabbit*; illus. by the author. New York: Warne, 1903.

Travers, Pamela. *Mary Poppins Opens the Door*; illus. by Mary Shepard and Agnes Sims. New York: Harcourt Brace Jovanovich, 1943, pages 97–98.

White, E. B. *Charlotte's Web*; illus. by Garth Williams. New York: Harper & Row, 1952, pages 43–44.

Wilder, Laura Ingalls. *The Little House in the Big Woods*; illus. by Garth Williams. New York: Harper & Row, 1953, pages 189, 193.

CHAPTER II. RHYTHM

ADULT REFERENCES

Cummings, E. E. *Chansons Innocentes, II*, in *Tulips & Chimneys*. New York: Liveright, 1976, page 25.

Shapiro, Karl. *Essay on Rime*. New York: Reynal and Hitchcock, 1945.

Sitwell, Edith. *A Poet's Notebook*. Westport, Conn.: Greenwood Press, 1950, page 187.

Whitman, Walt. "Preface to 1855 Edition, *Leaves of Grass*," in Miller, James E., Jr., *Complete Poetry and Selected Prose by Walt Whitman*. Boston: Houghton Mifflin, 1959, page 415.

Williams, William Carlos. "The Dance," in *The Collected Later Poems*. New York: New Directions, 1962, page 11.

CHILDREN'S BOOKS

De Regniers, Beatrice Schenk. *May I Bring a Friend?*; illus. by Beni Montresor. New York: Antheneum, 1964.

Fyleman, Rose R. "Husky Hi," in *Picture Rhymes from Foreign Lands*; illus. by Valery Carrick. Philadelphia: Stokes, 1935.

Gag, Wanda. *Millions of Cats*; illus. by the author. New York: Coward, McCann & Geoghegan, 1928.

Kipling, Rudyard. "The Elephant's Child" (see under Introduction in Bibliography).

Lindsay, Vachel. "The Potatoes' Dance," in *Johnny Appleseed and Other Poems*; illus. by George Richards. New York: Macmillan, 1960, pages 29-30.

McCloskey, Robert. *Centerburg Tales*; illus. by the author. New York: Viking Press, 1951.

Milne, A. A. *The House at Pooh Corner*; with decorations by Ernest H. Shepard. New York: Dutton, 1961, page 4.

SUPPLEMENTARY SUGGESTIONS

Arbuthnot, May H., and Root, Shelton L., Jr. *Time for Poetry*. Third edition; illus. by Arthur Paul. Chicago: Scott, Foresman, 1968.
Good general collection.

Cole, William, ed. *An Arkful of Animals*; illus. by Lynn Munsinger. Boston: Houghton Mifflin, 1978.
Poems that play with both sound and rhythm.

Hoberman, Mary Ann. *A Little Book of Little Beasts*; pictures by Peter Parnall. New York: Simon & Schuster, 1973.
Rhythmical poems in free forms.

McCord, David. *Far and Few*; drawings by Henry B. Kane. Boston: Little, Brown, 1952.
This poet is an acrobat with words and rhythms.

Milne, A. A. *When We Were Very Young*; illus. by Ernest H. Shepard. New York: Dutton, 1952.
"Halfway down" and "Hoppity" are good examples of use of the rhythm that is inherent in the content.

Oppenheim, Joanne. *Have You Seen Roads?*; illus. by Gerard Nook. Reading, Mass.: Addison-Wesley, 1969.
The right rhythm for each road.

Stevenson, Robert Louis. *A Child's Garden of Verses*; illus. by Jessie Willcox Smith. New York: Scribner, 1905.
See particularly "Windy Nights" for galloping rhythm, and "From a Railway Carriage" for train rhythm.

Welles, Winifred. *Skipping Along Alone*; illus. by Marguerite Davis. New York: Macmillan, 1931.
See particularly "Stocking Fairy" and "Old Ellen Sullivan" for rhythm matching mood.

Withers, Carl, compiler. *A Rocket in My Pocket: Rhymes and Chants of Young Americans*; illus. by Susanne Suba. New York: Holt, Rinehart & Winston, 1948.

CHAPTER III. SOUND

CHILDREN'S BOOKS

Andersen, Hans Christian. *Fairy Tales*; illus. by Jean O'Neill. Cleveland: Collins, 1975, page 275.

Farjeon, Eleanor. "Mrs. Peck Pigeon," from *Eleanor Farjeon's Poems for Children*. Philadelphia: Lippincott, 1951, page 108.

Grahame, Kenneth. *The Wind in the Willows* (see under Introduction in Bibliography), page 26.

Kipling, Rudyard. "How the Rhinoceros Got His Skin," in *Just So Stories*; illus. by the author and J. M. Gleeson. Garden City, N.Y.: Doubleday, 1912, page 39.

Milne, A. A. *The House at Pooh Corner* (see under Chapter II in Bibliography), page 95.

———. *When We Were Very Young* (see under Chapter II in Bibliography), page 33.

SUPPLEMENTARY SUGGESTIONS

Abercrombie, Barbara, ed. *The Other Side of a Poem*; art by Harry Bertschmann. New York: Harper & Row, 1977.
See especially the sections on "delicious sounds" and "music with words."

Burningham, John. *Mr. Gumpy's Outing*; illus. by the author. New York: Holt, Rinehart & Winston, 1971.
Full of words with playful sound effects.

Carroll, Lewis (pseud. of Charles Lutwidge Dodgson). *Alice's Adventures in Wonderland* and *Through the Looking Glass*; illus. by Sir John Tenniel, with an afterword by Clifton Fadiman. New York: Macmillan, 1963.
See particularly "The Jabberwocky," for suggestive use of sound.

Lear, Edward. *The Complete Nonsense Book*, ed. by Constance, Lady Strachey. New York: Dodd Mead, 1942.

Oxford Dictionary of Nursery Rhymes, ed. Opie, Iona, and Peter. Oxford: Oxford University Press, 1952.
See particularly the counting-out rhymes.

Richards, Laura. *Tirra Lirra; Rhymes Old and New*; illus. by Marguerite Davis. Boston: Little, Brown, 1955.
Outstanding for fun with words and sounds.

Rossetti, Christina. *Goblin Market*, illus. and adapted by Ellen Raskin. New York: Dutton, 1970.
Portions of this are particularly notable for sound quality.

Watson, Clyde. *Father Fox's Pennyrhymes*; illus. by Wendy Watson. New York: Crowell, 1979.
Exuberant word play and rhyming.

CHAPTER IV. FORM

CHILDREN'S BOOKS

Beskow, Elsa. *Pelle's New Suit*; illus. by the author, tr. from the Swedish by M. L. Woodburn. New York: Harper & Row, 1929.

Brown, Margaret Wise. *The Runaway Bunny*; illus. by Clement Hurd. New York: Harper & Row, 1972.

Burton, Virginia Lee. *Katy and the Big Snow*; illus. by the author. Boston: Houghton Mifflin, 1943.

Ets, Marie Hall. *In the Forest*; illus. by the author. New York: Viking Press, 1944.

Gag, Wanda. *Millions of Cats* (see under Chapter II in Bibliography).

———. *Tales from Grimm*; freely tr. and illus. by the author. New York: Coward, McCann & Geoghegan, 1936, page 151.

Kipling, Rudyard. "The Elephant's Child" (see under Introduction in Bibliography).

Paterson, Katherine. *The Great Gilly Hopkins*. New York: Crowell, 1978.

Potter, Beatrix. *The Tale of Peter Rabbit* (see under Chapter I in Bibliography).

For the nursery tales "The Little Red Hen," "The Three Little Pigs," "The Old Woman and Her Pig," and others outstanding for their repetitive or accumulative pattern, such as "The Gingerbread Boy," "The Three Bears," and "The House That Jack Built," see the following collections:

Haviland, Virginia, ed. *The Fairy Tale Treasury*; illus. by Raymond Briggs. New York: Coward, McCann & Geoghegan, 1972.

Hutchinson, Veronica S. *Chimney Corner Stories*; illus. by Lois Lenski. New York: Minton, 1925.

Jacobs, Joseph, ed. *English Folk and Fairy Tales*; illus. by J. D. Batten. New York: Putnam, n.d.

Rojankovsky, Feodor. *The Tall Book of Nursery Tales*; illus. by the author. New York: Harper & Row, 1944.

SUPPLEMENTARY SUGGESTIONS

Other folk tales that can be profitably studied for their patterned structures are "The Three Billy-Goats-Gruff" from the Scandinavian; "Drakestail" from the French; and "The Frog Prince," "The Hut in the Forest," and "One-Eye, Two-Eyes, and Three-Eyes," from Grimm. See the following:

Asbjörnsen, Peter Christen, and Moe, Jorgen E. *East of the Sun and West of the Moon*; ed. and illus. by Ingri and Edgar Parin d'Aulaire. New York: Viking Press, 1969.

Grimm, Jacob, and Grimm, Wilhelm. *Household Stories from the Collection of the Brothers Grimm*, tr. from the German by Lucy Crane and illus. by Walter Crane. New York: Dover Publications, 1963.

Lang, Andrew. *Red Fairy Book*; illus. by H. J. Ford and Lancelot Speed. New York: Dover Publications, 1966.

Modern stories, with a repetitive pattern construction, for preschool or early primary years:

Black, Irma Simonton. *Is This My Dinner?*; illus. by Rosalind Fry. Chicago: Whitman, 1972.

Brown, Margaret Wise. *Wait Till the Moon Is Full*; illus. by Garth Williams. New York: Harper & Row, 1948.

Charlip, Remy. *Fortunately*; illus. by the author. New York: Parents' Magazine Press, 1964.

De Regniers, Beatrice Schenk. *May I Bring a Friend?* (see under Chapter II in Bibliography).

Flack, Marjorie. *Ask Mister Bear*; illus. by the author. New York: Macmillan, 1958.

Skaar, Grace. *The Very Little Dog*; illus. by the author and Louise Woodcock. *The Smart Little Kitty*; illus. by Lucienne Bloch. Reading, Mass.: Addison-Wesley, 1947–49.

Thomas, Ianthe. *Lordy, Aunt Hattie*; illus. by Thomas di Grazia. New York: Harper & Row, 1973.

Tompert, Ann. *Little Fox Goes to the End of the World*; illus. by John Wallner. New York: Crown, 1976.

Tresselt, Alvin R. *Follow the Wind*; illus. by Roger Duvoisin. New York: Lothrop, Lee & Shepard, 1950.

Modern stories in the narrative style, for the early primary years:

Ardizzoni, Edward. *Little Tim and the Brave Sea Captain*; illus. by the author. New York: Walck, 1955.

Averill, Esther. *The Cat Club*; illus. by the author. New York: Harper & Row, 1944.

Boegehold, Betty. *Pippa Mouse*; illus. by Cindy Szekeres. New York: Knopf, 1973.

Charlip, Remy, and Supree, Burton. *Harlequin and the Gift of Many Colors*; illus. by Remy Charlip. New York: Parents' Magazine Press, 1973.

Flack, Marjorie. *The Story About Ping*; illus. by Kurt Wiese. New York: Viking Press, 1933.

Lattimore, Eleanor Frances. *Little Pear*; illus. by the author. New York: Harcourt Brace Jovanovich, 1931.

Steptoe, John. *Stevie*; illus. by the author. New York: Harper & Row, 1969.

CHAPTER V. CONTENT

ADULT REFERENCES

Briggs, Raymond. *The Snowman*. New York: Random House, 1978.

Carrighar, Sally. *One Day on Beetle Rock*; illus. by Henry B. Kane. Lincoln: University of Nebraska Press, 1978.

Carson, Rachel Louise. *The Sea Around Us*. New York: Oxford University Press, 1961.

James, Henry. "The Art of Fiction" in F. O. Matthiessen, *The James Family*. New York: Knopf, 1947, page 369.

———. *The Art of the Novel*. New York: Scribner, 1934, page 45.

CHILDREN'S BOOKS

Atwater, Richard and Florence. *Mr. Popper's Penguins*; illus. by Robert Lawson. Boston: Little, Brown, 1938.

Baum, L. Frank. *The Wizard of Oz*; illus. by W. W. Denslow. New York: Macmillan, 1970.

Brindze, Ruth. *The Gulf Stream*; illus. by Helene Carter. New York: Vanguard Press, 1945.

Brown, Margaret Wise. *The Quiet Noisy Book*; illus. by Leonard Weisgard. New York: Harper & Row, 1950.

Burton, Virginia Lee. *Mike Mulligan and His Steam Shovel*; illus. by the author. Boston: Houghton Mifflin, 1939.

———. *The Little House*; illus. by the author. Boston: Houghton Mifflin, 1942.

Clark, Mary E., and Quigley, Margery. *The Poppy Seed Cakes*, by Margery Clark (pseud.); illus. by Maud and Miska Petersham. Garden City, N.Y.: Doubleday, 1929.

Collodi, Carlo (pseud. of Carlo Lorenzini). *The Adventures of Pinocchio*; illus. by Fritz Kredel. New York: Grosset & Dunlap, 1946.

Estes, Eleanor. *The Hundred Dresses*; illus. by Louis Slobodkin. New York: Harcourt Brace Jovanovich, 1944.

———. *The Moffats*; illus. by Louis Slobodkin. New York: Harcourt Brace Jovanovich, 1968.

Ets, Marie Hall. *Play with Me*; illus. by the author. New York: Viking Press, 1955.

Flack, Marjorie. *Tim Tadpole and the Great Bullfrog*; illus. by the author. Garden City, N.Y.: Doubleday, 1959.

Fox, Frances Margaret. *The Little Cat Who Could Not Sleep*; illus. by Shirley Hughes. New York; Scroll Press, 1973.

Fritz, Jean. *Where Was Patrick Henry on the 29th of May?*; illus. by Margot Tomes. New York: Coward, McCann & Geoghegan, 1975.

Gag, Wanda. *Millions of Cats* (see under Chapter II in Bibliography).

Klein, Lenore. *Tom and the Small Ant*; illus. by Harriet Sherman. New York: Knopf, 1965.

Krauss, Ruth. *Bears*; illus. by Phyllis Rowland. New York: Harper & Row, 1948.

———. *The Carrot Seed*; illus. by Crockett Johnson. New York: Harper & Row, 1945.

———. *The Happy Day*; illus. by Marc Simont. New York: Harper & Row, 1949.

Lasky, Kathryn. *Tugboats Never Sleep*; illus. by Christopher G. Knight. Boston: Little, Brown, 1977.

Lawson, Robert. *Rabbit Hill*; illus. by the author. New York: Viking Press, 1944.

Lenski, Lois. *The Little Airplane*; illus. by the author. New York: Walck, 1938.

———. *The Little Auto*; illus. by the author. New York: Walck, 1934.

Milne, A. A. *The House at Pooh Corner* (see under Chapter II in Bibliography), page 108.

Minarik, Else Holmelund. *Little Bear*; illus. by Maurice Sendak. New York: Harper & Row, 1957.

———. *Little Bear's Visit*; illus. by Maurice Sendak. New York: Harper & Row, 1961.

Müller, Jörg. *The Changing City*. New York: Atheneum, 1977.

Paterson, Katherine. *The Great Gilly Hopkins* (see under Chapter IV in Bibliography).

Potter, Beatrix. *The Tale of Peter Rabbit* (see under Chapter I in Bibliography).

Rey, H. A. *Where's My Baby?*; illus. by the author. Boston: Houghton Mifflin, 1943.

Schneider, Herman and Nina. *How Big Is Big?*; illus. by A. F. Arnold. Reading, Mass.: Addison-Wesley, 1946.

———. *You, Among the Stars*; illus. by Symeon Shimin. New York: William R. Scott, 1951.

Slobodkina, Esphyr. *Caps for Sale*; illus. by the author. Reading, Mass.: Addison-Wesley, 1947.

Steig, William. *Caleb and Kate*; illus. by the author. New York: Farrar, Straus & Giroux, 1977.

————. *Sylvester and the Magic Pebble*; illus. by the author. New York: Simon & Schuster, 1969.

Treffinger, Carolyn. *Li Lun, Lad of Courage*; illus. by Kurt Wiese. Nashville: Abingdon Press, 1947.

Tresselt, Alvin R. *Autumn Harvest*; illus. by Roger Duvoisin. New York: Lothrop, Lee & Shepard, 1951.

————. *Hi, Mister Robin!*; illus. by Roger Duvoisin. New York: Lothrop, Lee & Shepard, 1950.

————. *Sun Up*; illus. by Roger Duvoisin. New York: Lothrop, Lee & Shepard, 1949.

————. *White Snow, Bright Snow*; illus. by Roger Duvoisin. New York: Lothrop, Lee & Shepard, 1947.

Wilder, Laura Ingalls. *By the Shores of Silver Lake*; illus. by Garth Williams. New York: Harper & Row, 1953.

————. *Farmer Boy*; illus. by Garth Williams. New York: Harper & Row, 1953.

————. *The Little House in the Big Woods* (see under Chapter I in Bibliography).

————. *The Little House on the Prairie*; illus. by Garth Williams. New York: Harper & Row, 1953.

————. *The Little Town on the Prairie*; illus. by Garth Williams. New York: Harper & Row, 1953.

————. *The Long Winter*; illus. by Garth Williams. New York: Harper & Row, 1953.

————. *On the Banks of Plum Creek*; illus. by Garth Williams. New York: Harper & Row, 1953.

————. *These Happy Golden Years*; illus. by Garth Williams. New York: Harper & Row, 1953.

Wright, Ethel. *Saturday Walk*; illus. by Richard Rose. Reading, Mass.: Addison-Wesley, 1954.

Zemach, Harve, and Zemach, Kaethe. *The Princess and Froggie*; illus. by Margot Zemach. New York: Farrar, Straus & Giroux, 1975.

CHAPTER VI. SOME COMMON PITFALLS

CHILDREN'S BOOKS

Baum, L. Frank. *The Wizard of Oz* (see under Chapter V in
  Bibliography).

Grahame, Kenneth. *The Wind in the Willows* (see under Introduction in Bibliography).

Lawson, Robert. *Rabbit Hill* (see under Chapter V in Bibliography).

Sendak, Maurice. *Where the Wild Things Are*; illus. by the author. New York: Harper & Row, 1963.

Spyri, Johanna. *Heidi*; intro. by Mary L. Becker; illus. by Leonard Weisgard. Cleveland: Collins, 1972.

Steig, William. *Sylvester and the Magic Pebble* (see under
  Chapter V in Bibliography).

Travers, Pamela. *Mary Poppins*; illus. by Mary Shepard. New
  York: Harcourt Brace Jovanovich, 1934.

SUPPLEMENTARY SUGGESTIONS

See the following for skillful bridging of the fantasy and reality worlds:

Carroll, Lewis (pseud. of Charles Lutwidge Dodgson). *Alice's
  Adventures in Wonderland* and *Through the Looking
  Glass* (see under Chapter III in Bibliography).

Cleary, Beverly. *The Mouse and the Motorcycle*; illus. by Louis
  Darling. New York: Morrow, 1965.

Gannett, Ruth Stiles. *My Father's Dragon*; illus. by Ruth Chris-
  man Gannett. New York: Random House, 1948.

Lewis, C. S. *The Lion, the Witch, and the Wardrobe*; illus. by
  Pauline Baynes. New York: Macmillan, 1970.

Seuss, Dr. (pseud. of T. S. Geisel). *The 500 Hats of Bartholo-
  mew Cubbins*; illus. by the author. New York: Vanguard
  Press, 1938.

Wells, Rosemary. *Morris's Disappearing Bag*; illus. by the author. New York: Dial Press, 1975.

White, E. B. *Charlotte's Web* (see under Chapter I in Bibliography).

EPILOGUE

ADULT REFERENCES

Bettelheim, Bruno. *The Uses of Enchantment: The Meaning and Importance of Fairy Tales.* New York: Knopf, 1976.

Lewis, C. S. *Out of the Silent Planet.* New York: Macmillan, 1943.

CHILDREN'S BOOKS

Bulychev, Kirill. *Alice*; tr. and adapted by Mirra Ginsburg; illus. by Igor Galanin. New York: Macmillan, 1977.

Cleary, Beverly. *Henry and the Clubhouse*; illus. by Louis Darling. New York: Morrow, 1962.

———. *Henry and the Paper Route*; illus. by Louis Darling. New York: Morrow, 1950.

———. *Henry and Ribsy*; illus. by Louis Darling. New York: Morrow, 1954.

———. *Ramona and Her Father*; illus. by Alan Tiegreen. New York: Morrow, 1977.

———. *Ramona the Brave*; illus. by Alan Tiegreen. New York: Morrow, 1975.

———. *Ramona the Pest*; illus. by Louis Darling. New York: Morrow, 1968.

Clifton, Lucille. *Everett Anderson's Christmas Coming*; illus. by Evaline Ness. New York: Holt, Rinehart & Winston, 1971.

———. *Everett Anderson's Friend*; illus. by Ann Grifalconi. New York: Holt, Rinehart & Winston, 1976.

———. *Everett Anderson's Nine Month Long*; illus. by Ann Grifalconi. New York: Holt, Rinehart & Winston, 1978.

———. *Everett Anderson's 1—2—3*; illus. by Ann Grifalconi. New York: Holt, Rinehart & Winston, 1977.

———. *Everett Anderson's Year*; illus. by Ann Grifalconi. New York: Holt, Rinehart & Winston, 1974.

———. *Some of the Days of Everett Anderson*; illus. by Evaline Ness. New York: Holt, Rinehart & Winston, 1970.

Ets, Marie Hall. *In the Forest*; illus. by the author. New York: Viking Press, 1944.

Goffstein, M. B. *Goldie the Dollmaker*; illus. by the author. New York: Farrar, Straus & Giroux, 1969.

Hoffman, Phyllis. *Steffie and Me*; pictures by Emily McCully. New York: Harper & Row, 1970.

Keats, Ezra Jack. *A Letter to Amy*; illus. by the author. New York: Harper & Row, 1968.

———. *Apt. 3*; illus. by the author. New York: Macmillan, 1971.

———. *Dreams*; illus. by the author. New York: Macmillan, 1974.

———. *Goggles*; illus. by the author. New York: Macmillan, 1969.

———. *Hi, Cat*; illus. by the author. New York: Collier Books, 1970.

———. *Louie*; illus. by the author. New York: Greenwillow Books, 1975.

———. *Pet Show!*; illus. by the author. New York: Macmillan, 1974.

———. *Peter's Chair*; illus. by the author. New York: Harper & Row, 1967.

———. *The Snowy Day*; illus. by the author. New York: Viking Press, 1962.

———. *Whistle for Willie*; illus. by the author. New York: Viking Press, 1964.

Lobel, Arnold. *Days with Frog and Toad*; illus. by the author. New York: Harper & Row, 1979.

———. *Frog and Toad All Year*; illus. by the author. New York: Harper & Row, 1976.

———. *Frog and Toad Are Friends*; illus. by the author. New York: Harper & Row, 1970.

———. *Frog and Toad Together*; illus. by the author. New York: Harper & Row, 1972.

Mathis, Sharon Bell. *The Hundred Penny Box*; illus. by Leo and Diane Dillon. New York: Viking Press, 1975.

Newfield, Marcia. *A Book for Jodan*; illus. by Diane de Groat. New York: Atheneum, 1975.

Peet, Bill. *The Wump World*; illus. by the author. Boston: Houghton Mifflin, 1970.

Sendak, Maurice. *Where the Wild Things Are* (see under Chapter VI in Bibliography).

Sonneborn, Ruth. *Friday Night Is Papa Night*; illus. by Emily McCully. New York: Viking Press, 1970.

Steig, William. *Amos & Boris*; illus. by the author. New York: Farrar, Straus & Giroux, 1971.

Steptoe, John L. *My Special Best Words*; illus. by the author. New York: Viking Press, 1974.

———. *Stevie* (see under Chapter IV in Bibliography).

———. *Train Ride*; illus. by the author. New York: Harper & Row, 1971.

———. *Uptown*; illus. by the author. New York: Harper & Row, 1970.

Tresselt, Alvin. *The Beaver Pond*; illus. by Roger Duvoisin. New York: Lothrop, Lee & Shepard, 1970.

———. *The Dead Tree*; illus. by Charles Robinson. New York: Parents' Magazine Press, 1972.

Viorst, Judith. *Alexander and the Terrible, Horrible, No Good, Very Bad Day*; illus. by Ray Cruz. New York: Atheneum, 1976.

White, E. B. *Charlotte's Web* (see under Chapter I in Bibliography).

Wiseman, B. *Bobby and Boo: The Little Spaceman*; illus. by the author. New York: Holt, Rinehart & Winston, 1978.

Yashima, Taro. *Crow Boy*; illus. by the author. New York: Viking Press, 1955.